T0247198

Love: A History in Five Fantasies

For Tom

Love: A History in Five Fantasies

Barbara H. Rosenwein

polity

Copyright © Barbara H. Rosenwein 2022

The right of Barbara H. Rosenwein to be identified as Author of this Work has been
asserted in accordance with the UK Copyright, Designs and Patents Act 1988.

First published in 2022 by Polity Press

Polity Press
65 Bridge Street
Cambridge CB2 1UR, UK

Polity Press
101 Station Landing
Suite 300
Medford, MA 02155, USA

ISBN-13: 978-1-5095-3183-7

A catalogue record for this book is available from the British Library.

Library of Congress Cataloging-in-Publication Data

Names: Rosenwein, Barbara H., author.
Title: Love : a history in five fantasies / Barbara H. Rosenwein.
Description: Cambridge, UK ; Medford, MA : Polity Press, 2021. | Includes
   bibliographical references and index. | Summary: "A learned guide through the
   labyrinth of love"-- Provided by publisher.
Identifiers: LCCN 2021012470 (print) | LCCN 2021012471 (ebook) | ISBN
   9781509531837 (hardback) | ISBN 9781509531868 (epub)
Subjects: LCSH: Love.
Classification: LCC BF575.L8 R68 2021 (print) | LCC BF575.L8 (ebook) | DDC
   152.4/1--dc23
LC record available at https://lccn.loc.gov/2021012470
LC ebook record available at https://lccn.loc.gov/2021012471

Typeset in 11 on 13 pt Sabon
by Cheshire Typesetting Ltd, Cuddington, Cheshire
Printed and bound in Great Britain by CPI Group (UK) Ltd, Croydon

For further information on Polity, visit our website:
politybooks.com

PHEBE: Good shepherd, tell this youth what 'tis to love.
SILVIUS: It is to be all made of fantasy,
   All made of passion and all made of wishes,
   All adoration, duty, and observance,
   All humbleness, all patience and impatience,
   All purity, all trial, all observance,
   And so am I for Phebe.

   William Shakespeare, *As You Like It*, Act V, scene 2

Contents

Acknowledgments

My first debt is to Riccardo Cristiani, with whom many of the topics considered here were first researched, discussed, and written up, albeit in other guises.

I thank seven insightful readers who offered exceptionally useful comments on the manuscript as a whole: Christian Bailey, Naomi Honeth, Frances Freeman Paden, Pascal Porcheron, Tom Rosenwein, Michael Sherman, and Peter N. Stearns. William D. Paden has always given me much to think about, and I am grateful for his comments on a version of chapter 4.

This project went through more changes than most, and in its various forms, including this one, I would gratefully like to acknowledge the help of many friends and colleagues beyond those already mentioned: Katie Barclay, Jan Burzlaff, Angelos Chaniotis, Jennifer Cole, Matthieu Dupas, Laura Fair, Kathryn de Luna, Leslie Dossey, Annalese Duprey-Henry, Dyan Elliott, Abram Van Engen, Nicole Eustace, Elina Gertsman, Frederic Wright Gleach, Adriana Laura Guarro, Susan Karant-Nunn, David Melton, Barbara Newman, Nancy Segal, Mark Seymour, Simon Swain, Lynn M. Thomas, Fabrizio Titone, Uwe Vagelpohl, and Ilona Wysmułek.

I thank Jennifer Stegen, a truly model interlibrary-loan librarian, and I am grateful for the fruitful partnership between the libraries of Loyola University Chicago and Northwestern University, which provided me with many extraordinary resources. At Polity Press, brilliant external readers, a very helpful staff, and above all Pascal Porcheron gave me much appreciated help and encouragement.

With love I thank my family: Jess and her girls, Sophie and Natalie; Frank and Amy and their boys Joshua, Julian, and Benji; and my sister, Naomi, who not only read the book in manuscript but also faithfully sent me emails throughout the thick and thin of this project. She and her husband, Jim, tolerated with good will my chatter via FaceTime about the ever-changing kaleidoscope that was this book in progress. I dedicate the finished product to my husband, Tom. Whatever the fantasies of love may be, he is it.

Note to Readers

All dates are CE (i.e. AD) unless otherwise noted; abbreviations associated with dates are d. = date of death, *c.* = circa (approximately), *fl.* = floruit (flourished). I have cited primary sources not originally in English in modern English translations. I have also updated the spelling and punctuation of early modern English materials and have in some instances substituted modern equivalents for outdated words and phrases. Unless otherwise noted, all biblical citations are from *The New Oxford Annotated Bible: New Revised Standard Version with the Apocrypha. An Ecumenical Study Bible*, ed. Michael D. Coogan with Marc Z. Brettler, Carol A. Newsom, and Pheme Perkins (5th edn, Oxford, 2018). All citations in both text and notes are to page number unless otherwise noted.

Introduction

I didn't always want to write a book on love. Perhaps I should have, for I was brought up in a household of committed Freudians, and Freud talked a lot about Eros. But under the spell of a wonderful college professor, Lester Little, I decided to become a historian of the Middle Ages. Given my upbringing, it was an odd decision. I tried to explain it to my parents by using what was then the lingo of my household: history is but the "manifest content" of the unconscious fantasies of the people living at the time. In other words, I was saying, history is the reported dream behind which is the *real* story. And I would discover that real story. I meant it. My favorite book at the time was Freud's *Interpretation of Dreams*.

I soon learned, however, how foolish my plan was for a nineteen-year-old, especially one who didn't yet know any Latin. I spent the next several decades working on languages, reading the sources, delving into the history – yes, the manifest content – of medieval history and particularly of medieval monasticism. But I retained my desire to understand what was "behind" the facts I was studying. Why did the most prestigious monks of the early Middle Ages – the Cluniacs – spend most of their time in church chanting psalms? What motivated pious laypeople at every level of society to give land to this

1

monastery? What notions of space and violence were behind the pope's declaration of a holy and inviolable circle around Cluny's properties? I drew on anthropology, sociology, and ethography; I gradually left Freud behind, though never entirely.

I wasn't interested in love then, not, at least, as a topic of study. Of course, as a kid, I thought about it. I had a best girlfriend; I had crushes; I had some really awful boyfriends who gave me great anguish and some very nice ones who gave me great joy until they didn't. But I met my husband, Tom, early on in college. We got married right after I graduated. We had twins, Frank and Jessica. I repeated, without thinking much about it, the chant of my generation: "Make love, not war." I didn't realize then that love is even more complicated than war.

Eventually my focus changed, and I became interested in the history of emotions. It began in 1995, when fellow medievalist Sharon Farmer asked me to chair a session at a meeting of the American Historical Association on "The Social Construction of Anger." As I listened to the papers and the discussion that ensued, it dawned on me that the history of emotions could be a way into that as yet unexplored material behind the "manifest content."

Certainly, the field was wide open for new research. The main paradigm for the history of emotions at that time was the "civilizing process" of sociologist Norbert Elias, who characterized the Middle Ages as an era of impulse, violence, and childish lack of socialization, ending only with the rise of the early modern absolutist state and its emphasis on impulse control and emotional restraint. I knew that he was wrong about the Middle Ages, and I suspected that he was wrong about the later periods. But I was not sure how to find my own approach.

So, I read – historical sources, theories of emotion, newly emerging paradigms of emotions' history. I was struck by the sheer variety of emotional norms and values practiced by different groups in the Middle Ages and beyond, and eventually I arrived at a way to think about these groups. They were (as I dubbed them) "emotional communities" – groups (often living at the same time, often equivalent to social communities) in which people share the same or similar valuations of particular emotions, goals, and norms of emotional expression. These communities sometimes overlap and borrow from one another, and they also may – generally do – change over time. Even so, they have enough in common to allow the researcher to study them as a coherent group.

I still wasn't particularly interested in love, except to note how each emotional community dealt with it – what or whom they loved; the value they placed on love; the ways in which they expressed it. But those questions were the same as the ones I asked of all the emotions: how they were expressed, celebrated, and devalued in any given emotional community. What I wanted to do, above all, was to track co-existing emotional communities during one particular slice of time and to see how new ones came to the fore and others receded in the ensuing eras.

So I wasn't much interested in individual emotions, although I did edit a collection of articles on anger in the Middle Ages, an outcome of the AHA panel on social construction.[1] And I did see the need for and interest in such studies. Even as I was writing about emotional communities in the Early Middle Ages, Joanna Bourke published a book on the history of fear and Darrin M. McMahon on happiness.[2] But those researchers were not interested in emotional communities. Bourke treated modern history and the ways in which our (primarily Anglophone) cultures use and abuse fear; McMahon was interested in Western ideas about happiness, not in Western emotions.

Eventually I found a way. First, I needed to expand my purview and write about a long span of time. That I accomplished in a book on emotional communities from 600 to 1700.[3] Only then could I write a book covering the story of one emotion over the long haul. I chose the topic of anger because it was both a virtue and a vice and thus more interesting to me than, say, joy. I organized the book by attitudes: some emotional communities abhorred anger; others considered it a vice but also (in limited ways) a virtue; still others argued that anger was "natural" and thus not fundamentally a moral issue; finally (and more recently) some celebrated anger and its energizing and violent possibilities.[4]

Only then did I turn to love. It, too, was an emotion about which almost no one agreed. I found it even more difficult and conflicted than anger. Consider these many contradictory truths, myths, memes and sayings about it:

- Love is good.
- Love is painful.
- Love hits like a thunderbolt.
- Love takes time and patience.
- Love is natural and artless.
- Love is morally uplifting and the foundation of society.
- Love is socially disruptive and must be tamed.
- Love is forever.
- Love is variety.
- Love is consummated in sex.
- Love is best when it is not sexual.
- Love transcends the world.
- Love demands everything.
- Love demands nothing.

All of these thoughts, reflections, and attitudes are seductive. All demand to be heard. No wonder that, at first, I had no idea how to write a history of love. Not only does (and did) it mean so many different things, but it also involves so many other emotions – joy, pain, wonder, confusion, pride, humility, shame, tranquility, anger. Then, too, it has a multitude of motives – wishes to control, to be dominated, to seduce, to be desired, to nurture, to be suckled. It may be used to justify actions – even conquest and war – that initially seem inimical to it.

As I read, however, I began to see some of the memes coalesce. They were fantasies, stories that recurred over and over, although in different guises and contexts. And, as I looked around me, I saw that they persisted even now, in modern stories – on TV, in novels, in movies – and in the lives of my friends and family. And I began to see, too, how these enduring fantasies of love had informed – and continued to influence – my own expectations of myself towards those I love and of them towards me.

Moreover, the purposes of these fantasies began to dawn on me. They were (and are) narratives that organize, justify, and make sense of experiences, desires, and feelings that are otherwise incoherent and bewildering. My family's revered authority, Dr. Freud, had long ago hinted at that same idea when he said that the symptoms of adult neurotics were the expressions of long-repressed infantile fantasies – complexes of feelings such as the one Freud called Oedipal and that he likened to the Greek myth.

But I need hardly appeal to Freud to understand that storytelling is a way to explain, organize, and master what people are feeling. Paradigmatic narratives are not just for children to try on, create, and then (possibly) act out. We can see their importance for adults, for example, in the work of sociologist Arlie Hochschild, though she was not talking about love. When Hochschild studied adherents of the American political right, she did not fully accept their manifest explanations of their political discontents, such as those that her affable informant Mike Schaff gave her: "I'm pro-life, pro-gun, pro-freedom to live our own lives as we see fit." She sought, rather, what she called the "deep story," the "feels-as-if story – it's the story feelings tell, in the language of symbols."[5] Mike and his compatriots' deep story went something like this: they were standing – had long been standing – in a line consisting mainly of white men like themselves, patiently waiting to arrive at the "American Dream," a dream of progress, economic betterment, and greater opportunities. They had suffered and worked long and hard to stand in that line. But interlopers – black, brown, immigrant – were cutting in front of them. Feelings of anger, shame, resentment, and pride all came together and made sense in this deep story. This is what I call a fantasy.

Such underlying fantasies are what L. E. Angus and L. S. Greenberg are thinking about, too, when they advocate psychotherapy that intervenes and changes the narratives that people use to understand their feelings and identities. They are the reasons why Iiro P. Jääskeläinen and his colleagues use neuroimaging to unravel "how narratives influence the human brain, thus shaping perception, cognition, emotions, and decision-making." They explain Joan Didion's striking essay opener: "We tell ourselves stories in order to live."[6]

The fact that the Western imagination – only one among many imaginations – has produced some fantasies of love that span the centuries does not mean that love is love, always has been, always will be. Some stories have had staying power, granted; but they nevertheless have always shifted shape, losing some meanings and taking on others. They serve as cultural referents, and they still exert a certain *frisson*, but they also always need updating. Consider a *New Yorker* cartoon by Maddie Dai featuring a damsel in distress, a mildly surprised dragon, and a knight in armor with sword in hand (see figure 1).[7] The narrative of the visual image – the knight has come to rescue the lady – is so familiar as to be almost part of our DNA. It is recycled (though never in exactly the old form) in Disney movies and childish daydreams. But the caption sabotages the expectations set up by the picture: the joke is that this particular knight is a modern guy. He queries the endangered lady about her reproductive desires and her financial philosophy before deigning to slay the dragon. Yet our laughter at the joke may be a bit bitter, for the idea that love implies self-sacrifice, that it is or should be unconditional, remains today an active ideal. In philosopher Simon May's view, "to its immense cost, human love has usurped a role that only God's love used to play."[8] This fantasy requires the impossible of human love, and yet it is a demand and expectation in some circles.

But not in all. And therein lie the emotional communities of love. For even as some people see "true love" to be patterned on Christ's gratuitous self-sacrifice, others understand it as an ecstatic experience that takes them beyond the earthly realm. And others adhere to still different enduring narratives of love. These fantasies and their transformations over time form the chapters of this book. Yet it is only their *entwined* histories that allow us to glimpse the many-faceted, indeed kaleidoscopic, history of love within the Western tradition because, to some degree, they always played off of one another – and because they are all available to us, however loyally we may adhere to one or the other.

Unlike some scientists today, I do not wish to claim what love *is*. Contrary to many philosophers, I have no idea what it should be. And, unlike intellectual historians, I do not want simply to survey past theories of love (though some of those theories do enter into my discussion). I want to understand what people think love is today and what they have thought it was in the past. I want to include women in the story. And I want to cite both "real" people and what they said about their loves alongside the fictions that so often provide the scaffolding for the fantasies of love that we elaborate and hang on to.

I have chosen five persistent narratives. In the first chapter, I take up the fantasy of like-minded love. I continue with love's transcendence – the notion that it takes us to a higher realm. Love as freedom as opposed to obligation is the subject of chapter 3, while chapter 4 confronts the fantasy that true love is obsessive and chapter 5 that it is insatiable. Each chapter is focused on a different modality and experience of love, all of which have long histories within the Western tradition. While they overlap at certain points, it may be said that like-mindedness has mainly to do with friendship, transcendence with love of God, obligation with marriages and other long-term erotic relationships, obsession with unrequited love, and insatiability with roaming.

Taken together, the threads here separated by theme form a richly hued tapestry. If it is as yet incomplete, that is as it should be, for the story of love, like love itself, is always in the process of change, re-elaboration, and new fantasy-making.

1

Like-Mindedness

In an early episode of the television tragi-comedy series *Enlightened*, the protagonist, Amy Jellicoe (played by Laura Dern), greets her friend Sandy (Robin Wright) with ecstatic joy. As they walk and talk together, Amy feels that in her friend she has found her soul-mate, her other self. She can tell her friend everything, and her friend immediately understands. In fact, she need not say a word, yet her friend will know her thoughts and feelings. In the end, sadly, Amy learns otherwise, as her friend has her own agenda, and it is not the same as Amy's.[1]

Dashed hopes, hurt feelings. Amy's desire to find "another self" did not have its roots in Sandy, who was simply a cipher, a relative unknown on whom Amy projected her hopes. Nor was it "hard wired" in Amy, as if an innate quality of the human (or female) psyche were to seek a soul-mate. Yet, even so, Amy's fantasy of finding another self was not invented by the series' script writers. Rather, those writers were building upon the shards of a seductive, consoling, and yet sometimes disappointing fantasy long embedded in the Western love tradition. The ideal of finding a soul-mate was constructed over time, in fits and starts, with ruptures, variants, luxuriant growths, and odd denials.

Partnerships

The idea is already in Homer's *Odyssey*, where like-mindedness signals absolute agreement. Homer (perhaps one person, perhaps a committee charged with reconciling various oral traditions, in any event writing around the eighth century BCE) recounted Odysseus' prolonged homecoming to Ithaca after defeating Troy. His story is essentially about flux and movement – ships sail, stall, and drift; waves crash; storms rage; men run, hide, and turn into pigs – until the hero at last returns to his one fixed center: the immovable nuptial bed at Ithaca that he built around the trunk of a deep-rooted olive tree. On that bed, after twenty years' absence and his wife's (Penelope's) twenty years of weeping, the two have "their fill of passionate lovemaking (*philótes*)" (23:300).[2]

Philótes, *philos*, and *philia* are ancient Greek words that suggest strong affection. Although some commentators say that in Homer there is only "obligation" and no possibility for the voluntary bonds of love and friendship, their theory breaks down precisely with the idea of "like-mindedness," where someone is "another self." Nestor, king of Pylos, speaks of one sort of like-mindedness when Telemachus (the son of Penelope and Odysseus) visits Pylos to seek news of his long-absent father. The old king tells Telemachus,

> The whole time noble Odysseus and I were out there
>   [battling Troy], neither
> in council nor in assembly did we oppose each other,
> but, being of one mind, with good plans and shrewd
>   judgment
> we'd counsel the Argives [the Greek troops] on their
>   best course of action. (3:126–9)

Nestor insists on offering every hospitality to Telemachus, showing him both respect and affection. Nevertheless, his being "of one mind" with Odysseus was clearly very different from Amy's sense that all her hopes and dreams were shared by her friend. Nestor was referring to political agreement: he and Odysseus had the same plans, the same good counsel for their armies. This was limited like-mindedness. Even so, it engendered an affection that extended to the next generation.

Homer described a more profound like-mindedness in the counsel that Odysseus gave to the young and beautiful Nausicaa, a princess who offered hospitality to the hero when he was shipwrecked on her shores. She was attracted to him and wanted to marry him. But he was determined to return home. Instead of himself, he offered her a blessing:

> May the gods grant you all that your heart desires,
> husband, home, and like-mindedness – a precious gift,
> for there's nothing greater or better, ever, than when
>   two
> like-minded people are keeping house together,
> a man and his wife. (6:180–4)

"Two like-minded people keeping house together" was the foundation of Odysseus' own marriage, and the relationship of Nestor and Odysseus paled in its shadow. Only a man and a woman could keep house together with like mind. Odysseus and Penelope were *ekluon* – "they listened and heard and paid attention to each other."[3] Yet their like-mindedness, too, was not quite like Amy's because theirs was of the flesh, with love-making at its core. At the same time, it was practical, involving the pursuit of common goals by two people in utter harmony and agreement. And so, after Odysseus returned home, after the two had made love, Odysseus told Penelope:

> But now we've come at last to the marriage bed we
>   yearned for,

you'll care for such possessions as I have here in the
    halls;
and as for the flocks that these haughty suitors have
    wasted [as they wooed Penelope in Odysseus' very
    palace],
I'll get a good many by raiding, and others that the
    Achaians [Odysseus' countrymen]
will give me, until we've replenished every last empty
    stall! (23:354–8)

For those of us harboring the fantasy (we shall look
closely at it in chapter 4) of obsessive love, this seems
like an anti-climax: this man has been away from his
wife for twenty years, and nevertheless he tells her that
he will soon take off again to go raiding. But it makes
perfect sense in the context of Homeric like-mindedness, the joint pursuit of what is best for "keeping
house" – the economic and political as well as the erotic
unit.

In this ancient fantasy of love and like-mindedness,
the man calls the shots. He tells Penelope to "care for
the possessions in the halls." Is she really of like mind?
He tells Nausicaa what marriage is about. Does she see
it that way? The male prerogative is here so built in that
Homer would not have been conscious of it.

*

But, four centuries later, Plato was very aware of the
disparity of power between people in love, especially
in erotic love. In Plato's Athens, Eros was associated
above all with pederasty – not the same thing as pedo-
philia, with which it is often confused. Pederasty was a
relationship justified by an adolescent boy's need to be
educated – intellectually, militarily, and morally – by an
older man. The idea was to instruct the boy in virtue,
in the qualities and knowledge needed for a citizen of
the city-state, and, yes, to engage in sex, though gener-

ally non-penetrative. The boy was expected to be a bit shy, even rather unwilling; the older man was to be the wooer and the lover. Plato was well aware of the unequal power involved in this set-up. That helps explain why, when he wrote the *Laws* (one of his last dialogues), he made *chaste* friendships rather than sexual liaisons the foundation of social and political harmony.[4] When sex is involved, one or the other partner will dominate, and that will destroy the equality needed for a flourishing citizenry. In the *Laws*, Plato looked to non-erotic friendships to supply the like-mindedness that would give the state its own rock-solid foundation. He had in mind people who were equals politically, who cared for one another's well-being, and who were like-minded above all in their mutual and life-long pursuit of virtue. He made no room for like-minded husbands and wives. The marital unit was useful only for procreation and to channel sexual passion.

But in other dialogues Plato outlined different solutions to the inequality that seemed built into erotic relationships. His most compelling argument came in his *Symposium*. Named for the stag parties (*symposia*) common in classical Greek city-states, these get-togethers featured flute girls, lots of wine, and good conversation. Plato's *Symposium* brought together (fictively) a number of luminaries from an earlier generation, including Socrates. Dismissing the flute girls, the men decide not to get drunk but, rather, to offer improvised speeches in praise of Eros, god of love. The speech that Plato gives to the comic playwright Aristophanes solves the problem of inequality in sexual relations by making love the search for one's "other half."

Originally, says Aristophanes, humans were perfectly round in shape and utterly self-sufficient, needing no one else. They were (in a way) two in one: some two men, others two women, still others a man and a woman. Each had two faces, two genitals, four legs, four arms. They could move very fast by cartwheeling, and they were so proud of themselves that they "made an attempt on the gods" (190b).[5] For this intolerable hubris, Zeus cut them in half and had Apollo sew them up and turn their heads around, so that they would face their cut half, which Apollo smoothed out, except for "a few wrinkles around the stomach and the navel" (191a). That cut was a most miserable solution, for each of the halves spent all their days seeking their other half and trying to regrow together. They thought of nothing else, and so everyone was dying, no one was reproducing, and the gods were not getting their due worship and sacrifice from humans.

Then Zeus hit on another solution: he moved all the genitals to the front – to the wounded side – and henceforth, "when a man embraced a woman, he would cast his seed and they would have children; but when male embraced male, they would at least have the satisfaction of intercourse" (191c). And the women "split from a woman . . . are oriented more towards women" (191e). Although it was not absolutely certain that everyone would find their other half, Aristophanes focused on the joy that resulted when they did meet: "something wonderful happens: the two are struck from their senses by love." After that, they "finish out their lives together" (192c). Aristophanes' story made like-minded love the only true form of love altogether. Sex was the least important part: "No one would think . . . that mere sex is the reason each lover takes so great and deep a joy in being with the other." Rather, love was the longing of soul for soul. Lovers "don't want to be separated from one another, not even for a moment" (192c). They would be glad to "melt together," rather like soldiers in the ideal Greek phalanx (192e). With his idea of divided wholes, Aristophanes solved the problem of sexual inequality: if couples were halves of each other, then, even in sex, they wielded exactly the same power.

No one at the dinner party directly criticized Aristophanes. But they all were so eager to present their own very different takes on love that we might wonder if his radical assertion of the equality of genders rubbed against ancient prejudices.

Certainly, that was the case in the generation following Plato, as we see in the writings of Aristotle (d. 322 BCE), a student of Plato but far more orderly, pragmatic, and earthbound. Aristotle confined the idea of "another self" to male friends and, even then, only to friends of the very best sort, men who bonded because they were equally virtuous. Aristotle was very aware of lesser forms of friendships: people who expected favors from one another or who simply enjoyed being together. Those were good friendships as far as they went, and for all of them he used the term *philia*, love in the general sense of affection. But the best friendships – "complete" friendships, Aristotle called them – involved men who were virtuous and who wished the best for each other. Virtue was hard won. It meant, in a nutshell, developing one's full capabilities as a human being under the guidance of reason. No one was born virtuous, and only freeborn males who had the right sort of upbringing and education could ever hope to be so. Moreover, virtuous thought and behavior had to be exercised over and over, in every situation, in order to become habitual: that, alone, was the sign of true virtue. Thus, virtuous men were rare, and if they became complete friends (something that took time to develop) they wanted to spend all their days together, sharing their "enjoyments and distresses" – their various triumphs and setbacks – as they pursued virtue together (1171a5).[6] It was a joyful, if arduous, vocation. Children couldn't undertake it because their reason was as yet undeveloped; women might do so only under the guidance of the superior reason of a man – a father, a husband. There was no notion here of cultivating separate individualities; in their pursuit of virtue, friends had the same goal. That was the sense in which Aristotle could assert that "a friend is another self" (1170b).

It is true that Aristotle observed mothers who wanted the best for their children, sharing their sorrows and joys and sacrificing themselves and their own desires for the sake of their progeny. Such mothers were *like* "complete" friends to their offspring, but not quite, for complete friendships demanded reciprocity, and children could never reciprocate equally. But husbands might do so. Then could husbands and wives be like-minded? Yes, but only in the way Odysseus and Penelope were "on the same page" even though they did not mirror each other, Penelope taking care of their home, Odysseus out raiding to replenish their stock. Thus, Aristotle admitted, the "friendship [of husbands and wives] seems to include both utility and pleasure. And it may also be friendship for virtue, if they are decent" (1162a20–5). That's as close as he got to calling the conjugal couple like-minded.

*

The ancient Greeks thus gave a grudging nod to the possibility that women might be of like mind with another man or another woman. But when the notion of "another self" turned up at Rome in the severe writings of orator, politician, and moralist Cicero (d. 43 BCE), women were rigorously excluded. Why even bring up Cicero, then, in a discussion of the historical fragments on which one modern fantasy of love is constructed? It is partly because Cicero's dialogue *On Friendship* made so clear the connections between love and certain expectations of self-mirroring that we cannot leave it out. It is also because Cicero's work was endlessly mined, its golden aphorisms repurposed for every occasion and context. Finally, it is because we might, however reluctantly, forgive Cicero his sexism, since he could not imagine friendships separated from the political sphere – where Roman women had no place. But, in fact, most Roman *men* had no political role either, even in the late Republican period in which Cicero lived and worked. Only elite men (and a few upstarts like Cicero himself) could be involved in late Roman Republican politics. And so Cicero made friendships, too, the privilege of a small male elite "abundantly blessed with wealth and power." And then he added "and especially virtue," narrowing the possibilities even more (14.51).[7]

For Cicero, friendship begins only when a man of upright morals (already a tall order) sees or hears about another who is worthy of his admiration. Then the upright man cannot help but feel "love and kindly affection" towards that praiseworthy model of virtue. He longs to be nearer to his ideal; he bends ever closer, like a plant seeking the sun (9.32). If he is lucky, a "close intimacy" becomes possible, and when the admirer and the admired render each other kindly services and do things together, then, "joined to the soul's first impulse to love, there springs up . . . a marvelous glow and greatness of goodwill" (9.29). "Goodwill" – *benevolentia* in Latin – is a lusterless word in English. Think of it in Italian, then, where it still carries some of its Latinate passion: *ti voglio bene*, "I love you": it's the sort of love that you feel for your dearest friends, your parents, and your children. It's a lovely, warm feeling, though it brings with it a train of anxieties, for you care and you worry and you grieve when something amiss happens to those you love.

We might expect that the ordinarily Stoic Cicero would, as usual, shrink from the emotions of friendship, for he considered feelings to be unwelcome and uncomfortable mental disturbances. But friendship was an exception, and, in its favor, Cicero became an eloquent defender of feelings. Without affection, he dared to declare, there would be no difference "between a man and a stock or a stone" (13.48).

18

In his dialogue *On Friendship*, he made Laelius (who had lived several generations before him) his model and spokesman. Laelius, as Cicero depicted him, basked in the warm glow of his friendship with the great general Scipio Africanus. Even after Scipio had passed away, Laelius took comfort "in the recollection of our friendship." He counted himself a happy man because his life "was spent with Scipio, with whom I shared my public and private cares; lived under the same roof at home; served in the same [military] campaigns abroad, and enjoyed that wherein lies the whole essence of friendship – the most complete agreement in policy, in pursuits, and in opinions" (4.15).

These words are close to those of Nestor when he described his relationship with Odysseus. But the friendship of Laelius and Scipio was still stronger, for they had actually lived together and shared their intimate joys and sorrows. Did they have sex together too? It is possible, for, as Craig Williams' careful study of the topic suggests, free-born Roman males did not consider same-sex desire to be problematic, nor, in certain cases, did they disapprove of same-sex acts.[8] But in the course of the dialogue Laelius makes a great fuss about the need for equality between friends (19.69); if he and Scipio had sex together, only one of them could (as the Romans understood the matter) have taken the "masculine," penetrative role. So, it is unlikely that Laelius' invocation of "complete agreement" included sex.

What it did include, however, was such utter like-mindedness that, as Cicero put it, a friend "is, as it were, another self." We love ourselves because we care about ourselves, and we become attached to others about whom we care. That's why a human being "uses his reason to seek out another whose soul he may so mingle with his own as almost to make one out of two!" (21.80–1).

This may sound a bit like Aristophanes, but Cicero's "mingling" had nothing to do with sex, and his emphasis on "reason" was utterly foreign to the Aristophanean experience of love. Above all, that experience was joyful, whereas Cicero's was closer to pain. This was in part due to contexts: in the *Symposium*, Plato was putting words into the mouth of a comic playwright. Cicero, however, was thinking of real friends and his own perilous political position. Indeed, even as he was writing his dialogue on friendship, he was trying to decide whether to support Octavian or Antony as they vied for control over the government of Rome. Cicero opted for Octavian, but, when the two would-be dictators agreed to work together, they also agreed to sacrifice their former "friends" and family members. Cicero was among the "proscribed" and condemned to death. Under such circumstances, it took either a very brave man or a very foolish one to "mingle" his soul with another's in all things rather than save his own neck. That's why Cicero worried about how far loyalty to a friend should go. Not so far, Cicero said, as to do something wrong when your friend asks it of you.

Above all, Ciceronian friendships were melancholy precisely because so much was expected of them, and rarely could they deliver all. Cicero loved to be with Atticus, his friend from boyhood and the man to whom he dedicated *On Friendship*. "There are many things to worry and vex me, but once I have you here to listen, I feel I can pour them all away in a single walk and talk." But Atticus was not "here to listen"; in fact, he was rarely in Italy, preferring to live as a gentleman of leisure on his estates far off in Greece. Cicero mourned his absence: "You whose talk and advice has so often lightened my worry and vexation of spirit, the partner in my public life and intimate of all my private concerns, the sharer of all my talk and plans, where are you?"[9] Friendship was supposed to bring enormous pleasure; but we see here how it often brought sorrow and longing.

God as the glue

It was precisely the pains of such love that Christians came to belittle. They had a better, more permanent object of love: God. Once the Roman Empire became Christian, at the end of the fourth century CE, Cicero's world-tethered sort of friendship could not remain the ideal. Nor could Cicero's political career. Now Rome had a single ruler, an emperor. The kinds of men who used to go down to the Forum to debate state policy now sat in episcopal seats and worried about their pastoral duties, or they advocated on behalf of thorny theological questions at Church councils.

Augustine (d. 430), bishop of Hippo and paramount Church Father of the West, knew Cicero's *On Friendship* well. Indeed, before he converted to Christianity, he had had a friend in the Ciceronian mold: a childhood soul-mate, someone with whom he shared enthusiasms, someone from whom he never wanted to be apart. When his friend died young, Augustine's reaction was nothing like Scipio's tranquil reminiscing. Instead, he was beside himself with grief, "surprised that other mortals could remain alive when the man, whom I had loved as though he would never die, was dead." He could not believe that he, "who was his other self," still lived. He wished he might die, "for I felt that my soul and my friend's had been one soul in two bodies. . . . I did not want to live as a half being" (4.6).[10]

To stanch his painful awareness of love's sorrows, Augustine found an extraordinary solution: he denied that his love had been "real." The sort of friendship he had enjoyed was a sham, "because there can be no true friendship unless those who cling to each other are welded together by you" (4.4). The "you" here is God.

Augustine declared friendship to be a triad (see figure 2). Like Laelius, he agreed that friendship begins when a man of virtue is drawn towards another of the same character, but Augustine's "man of virtue" is a Christian drawn *by God* to another Christian. God is the glue that holds them together. When Augustine hears of a man who has suffered for his Christian beliefs, "I am eager to be united with him, to make myself known to him, and to bind him to myself in friendship. . . . I approach him, address him, engage him in conversation, express my affection for him; . . . and in turn I wish that the same affection should be brought about in him and expressed towards me" (9.11).[11] But what if this man has the wrong ideas about God? Then Augustine's love cannot hold. In short, the definition of "like mind" has here narrowed to "like belief." This is the beginning of identity politics. In Augustine's case, it means using force, if need be, against those who do not share his beliefs. He defends this as "love mingled with severity."[12] We shall see more of it in chapter 2.

*

Augustine's age was "transitional" in the sense that, in the ensuing thousand years or so, Catholic Christianity was (despite many exceptions) a given in most of Europe; people could be friends with fair certainty that they shared the same beliefs. In the eleventh and twelfth centuries – with urban centers springing up, new schools burgeoning, and classical models gaining new purchase – the idea of love as the search for "another self" gained in popularity. It often turned up in letters between male teachers and students, a presumably desexualized version of Greek pederasty. Typical was one anonymous schoolmaster who replied to a letter from one of his charges with words of passion: "Hardly had my ears, wide open and tensed with expectation, taken in the news that your life, which is my own, and your affairs, which I regard as mine, were secure . . . when at once my soul was suffused with . . . joy." Erotic language, so potent in many other medieval love fantasies, as we shall see, entered this discourse as well: "how much greater, how much fuller [will be my joy] when you will enrich me with your bodily presence, and I rejoice to embrace you and speak with you, exult in this joy, and my whole body dances inwardly!"[13]

Similar sentiments suffused some male–female relationships. *The Book of Encouragement and Consolation* by the monk Goscelin of Saint-Bertin (late eleventh century) was addressed to one Eva, a young nun for whom he had served as spiritual advisor.[14] The two now far apart (she in France, he in England), he wrote "to his only soul." Their special relationship was, he claimed, guaranteed by Christ: "This secret between two people is sealed with Christ as mediator, offering in sacrifice nothing but virginal simplicity and pure love." He assured Eva that there was no "scandal" in his thoughts and feelings. Some commentators have claimed that he protested too much. What is clear is that he was embroidering on the fantasy first articulated by Aristophanes and elaborated by Augustine: Christ had separated Goscelin from Eva "in body," but soon, in heaven, God "will refashion as a single soul what used to be one soul in two people." Like the spherical man when first cut in half, Goscelin moans and sobs – but he Christianizes his longing: it is for his "soulmate." Christianized too are his and Eva's progeny: he writes that he had not given Eva children but, rather, the desire for Christ. (We see here a glimmer of the dream of transcendence that we shall explore in the next chapter: reproduction not in flesh but, rather, in something greater and higher.) Taking advantage of the feminine gender of the word *anima*, soul, Goscelin sometimes speaks of himself as

Eva's mother, invoking his "maternal" care for his daughter. But that daughter has disappointed him. Eva left her English nunnery hastily, without saying good-bye to him. That "oversight" wounded Goscelin cruelly. In his *Book*, he laments and chides her. Even so, he praises her for seeking out a stricter kind of enclosure in France than she had had in her English nunnery, and he looks to her superior virtue to intercede with God to bring about their heavenly union. The seductive fantasy of oneness disappoints in this world, but Christianity offers the hope that it will come to fruition in the next.

In this charged atmosphere of impassioned masters and students, monks and nuns (which played out in numerous contexts), it is not surprising that Cicero's *On Friendship* was rewritten to suit the times. *Spiritual Friendship* was a late work by Aelred (d. 1167), abbot of the English Cistercian monastery of Rievaulx. Modeled on Cicero's dialogue, it featured Aelred himself in earnest conversation with a few other monks about true friendship "in Christ" (1.8).[15] Like a conservative U.S. Supreme Court justice, Aelred was determined to begin with "original intent." What had been the Creator's initial plan? To Aelred, it was clear: when God made the world, he impressed upon it his own unity. Thus, even stones are not "one of a kind" but abide together in a stream, evincing "a kind of love of companionship" (1.54). How much more truly, then, did God create mankind as a social being, a lover of others! But, with the Fall, people split into two groups. The worldly practice a love that is grasping and eager for gain. The righteous, by contrast, understand that they must love even their enemies. Nevertheless, they reserve a more precious sort of love for friends,

> with whom you may talk as freely as with yourself, to whom you neither fear to confess any fault nor blush at revealing any spiritual progress, to whom you may

entrust all the secrets of your heart and confide all your plans. And what is more delightful than so to unite spirit to spirit and so to make one out of two that there is neither fear of boasting nor dread of suspicion? (2.11)

The "spirit" that unites us with another comes from Christ, who inspires (literally, in-spirits) "the love with which we love a friend" (2.20). The next step in that rarified sequence arrives when Christ offers his very self to us as our friend. Then we join our spirit to Christ's – not physically (as we do when we offer the kiss of peace to other people in church), not even spiritually (as we do when we love our human friend), but intellectually, "with all earthly attachments calmed and all worldly thoughts and desires lulled" (2.27).

Not just Cicero but the Bible as well encouraged these ideas: the love of Jonathan and David in 1 Samuel 20:17; the mutual love of the members of the first apostolic community, which "was of one heart and one soul" (Acts 4:32); Jesus' command to "love one another as I have loved you. . . . You are my friends" (John 15:12–17). While Cicero had been worried that love might lead a man to do something dishonorable for a friend, Aelred considered that outcome impossible by the very definition of true friendship: it had always to be among virtuous people and thus could never require anything disgraceful. Of course, a friend might be imperfect; he might be (say) irascible. In that case, if no high moral principle were at stake, one might bend one's will a bit to conform to the will of that irascible friend. Here was an unusual concession – the idea that we might have to adjust to one another. Once we have accepted a person as our friend – something that (as Aelred stressed) must not be done lightly – we must tolerate the times when he is decidedly *not* our other half. This view had the potential to stave off disappointments.

Women's "other selves"

How like-minded was Penelope to Odysseus in fact? What did Eva think of Goscelin's book of praise and blame? What did women make of all these protestations of other selves?

We may say something about that at least in the instance of Heloise, romantic partner and then wife of Abelard (d. 1142). The two lovers were both brilliant intellectuals, the products of extraordinary educations in both classical and biblical literature. The story of their affair is well known. Abelard himself told it his way in his *Calamities*, written fifteen or so years after the couple had parted to join separate religious houses. As he said, he had been a celebrated philosopher and was therefore hired to put the finishing touches on the education of Heloise, niece of Parisian canon Fulbert. Teacher and student fell in love (in his *Calamities*, Abelard said that he simply wanted to seduce her), and Heloise became pregnant. Given the Church's strictures against sex outside of marriage and the fact that schoolmen like Abelard were in holy orders (and thus expected to be celibate), marriage could have ruined his career. More strikingly, Heloise didn't want to marry, chafing against the idea of contract and obligation (see chapter 3) rather than love freely given. Abelard's solution was to wed in secret. It didn't work. After they married, the two kept the secret by hardly seeing each other. Fulbert, who knew of the marriage, thought that Abelard had abandoned his niece and ordered his kinsmen to castrate Abelard. Thereafter the two separated, each taking monastic vows. Their son, Astralabe, was raised by Abelard's sister.

We know a lot about their feelings from their letters, which consist of two sets: the best known were written after Abelard published his *Calamities*, the lesser known composed as their affair unfolded.[16] In these letters – all

carefully worded and often in Latin verse, not only to
arouse the admiration of the beloved but also probably with an eye to future publication – both lovers
employed the trope of "another self." Heloise (let us
concentrate on her) appropriated that hitherto largely
male idea and made it her own. Some of her uses were
fairly derivative, like the opening of her letter to Abelard
at the very start of their affair: "To him who shines
bright with all virtues and holds more delight than the
honeycomb: his most faithful one of all gives herself, the
other half of his soul, in all faithfulness" (Newman 97).
She is the "other half of his soul": nothing new here. It
was the conceit of Aristophanes and, closer to Heloise's
time, the image used by Goscelin of Saint-Bertin, who
wrote (as we have seen) of God's refashioning "as a
single soul what used to be one soul in two people." But
in Heloise's letters another idea soon appears that colors
many of her protestations of like-mindedness, giving
them a peculiar cast. For, in order to ensure that both
she and Abelard will wish exactly the same thing, she
vows to obey him in everything. In one letter, she offers
an almost programmatic statement. Beginning with a
quasi-Ciceronian definition of friendship, she considers
how she may make theirs absolutely watertight: "What
love is, what it can do – I too have been intuitively
reflecting on this. Having perceived the likeness of our
character and concerns – a thing that especially con-
solidates friendships and reconciles friends – I would
repay you in exchange by loving and obeying you in
all things" (Newman 118). She sees like-mindedness in
their "character and concerns." This is the foundation
of their love. It carries an obligation, an idea that we
shall explore more fully in chapter 3. But while in that
chapter obligation tends to mean conforming to certain
role expectations, here it signifies an ongoing exercise
of sheer will: "You know, my heart's beloved, that the
duties of true love are rightly fulfilled only when they

are owed without ceasing, so that we do everything in our strength for the beloved, yet do not cease to will beyond our strength" (Newman 119). Do everything for the beloved? Aelred was willing to bend a bit; Heloise is ready to knuckle under, and "without ceasing."

These claims were neither idle nor theoretical. Heloise did indeed obey Abelard, even against her "own will," which, however, she submerged into his own. She did not want to marry him – liking far better to be called his "whore" than his "wife," since it would prove that she wanted nothing but "you yourself, never a marriage, never a dowry, never any pleasure, any purpose of my own" (Levitan 55). But wed him she did because he ordered it. When he told her to take monastic vows, she complied, although she had no such vocation at all. As she confessed, "It was not any commitment to the religious life that forced me to the rigors of the convent when I was the young woman I once was: it was your command alone. . . . I can expect no reward from God since it is clear I have yet done nothing out of love for him." Indeed, she avowed, she would have jumped into the raging fires of Hell if Abelard had told her to do so: "I would have followed you to Vulcan's flames if you commanded it, and without a moment's hesitation I would have gone first" (Levitan 60–1).

But, if Heloise was willing to drown her ego in Abelard's, she expected no less from him – and was bitterly disappointed that he did not see things that way as well. When she entered the monastery and "foundered overwhelmed in sorrow day after day," he never once tried to console her, "and yet [she upbraided him] you would know that you are bound to me by a greater debt [than all the Church Fathers who comforted women in religious orders], obliged to me by the sacrament of marriage, and beholden to me further by what is plain to everyone: that I have always held you in my heart with a love that has no measure." This was a debt that

Abelard owed her, he alone, "now above all, when I have so completely fulfilled your commands" (Levitan 54–5).

Here was the catch to Odysseus' blessing for Nausicaa, that there is "nothing greater or better, ever, than when two like-minded people are keeping house together." Arriving at that like-mindedness requires sacrifices. Cicero knew this: when he warned that friendship would have to end where dishonor began, he was willing, in effect, to accept that some loves might end in divorce. Aelred thought that Christ-inspired friendship meant that neither friend would (or could) do or ask anything disgraceful, but he admitted that sometimes he had to agree with his irascible friend just to maintain their relationship. And then there was Heloise, Abelard's "friend," so like him "in character and concerns"; she devoted her life to maintaining that likeness, whatever the cost. Was there nothing greater or better, as Odysseus put it? Heloise would have agreed with Odysseus. True, she upbraided Abelard for not caring for her and her monastic community; she wanted him to share in her responsibilities. In the end Abelard listened to her and took on the role of religious director for the convent that she presided over.

From Heloise's point of view, the beautiful Odyssean dream of perfect accord in all things will work only if there is a lot of self-sacrifice on the part of both partners. And perhaps that was Homer's point as well. The *Odyssey* may be seen as the story of a husband laboring to return home while his wife does her best to maintain it intact. Only because they had both done their parts could they achieve at last their like-minded unity.

*

The dilemmas faced by Abelard and Heloise ended when, in the sixteenth century, the medieval Church shattered into various Christian confessions. The chaste life lost its cachet in Protestant realms, and ambitious young men went to fight in war or (much the same thing) engaged in aggressive enterprises – settlement, trade, conquest – in Africa, the Americas, and Asia. Or, if they could afford it, they devoted themselves to their landed estates and wrote (as wealthy Romans like Cicero had once done) in their spare time. And young women? They wed. Or (as we shall see) they did not, aspiring to be writers themselves.

This was the world of Michel de Montaigne (d. 1592) when he met Étienne de La Boétie. Their friendship, he later wrote, was one of a kind, inexplicable, so rare that its like could hardly be established "once in three centuries."[17] It was so perfect that their two wills merged:

> It is no one special reason, nor two, three, four, nor a thousand; it is I know not what quintessence of the entire mixture that, having captured my entire will, brought it to plunge and lose itself in his; and that, once it captured all his will, brought it to plunge and be lost in mine with a like hunger, a like convergence.

The two were so fused that "neither of us reserved anything for ourself – nothing was either his or mine." Generalizing from his experience with La Boétie, Montaigne wrote that "the union of such friends, being truly perfect, makes them ... hate and avoid any words of division and distinction between them: benefit, obligation, gratitude, request, thanks, and the like." Everything they have belongs to the other: "wills, thoughts, opinions, goods, wives, children, honor, and life." Wives and children? This goes beyond anything we have seen before. Given that, Montaigne's idea that the two were "but one soul in two bodies" seems almost banal.

Both Montaigne and La Boétie came from the same general region of southwest France; were equally well-to-do and educated; served together as counsellors in the Parlement of Bordeaux for some years. Their friendship lasted a short time, for La Boétie died young. Montaigne, shaken, "made myself fall in love," married, and soon retired from the Parlement to take up (as he claimed) a life of calm study.[18] (It didn't work, and he may not have wanted it to. In any event, he was often called upon for public service in this time of tumultuous religious wars in France.) He began to write essays about himself and his experiences, perhaps as a sort of substitute for writing letters to the deceased La Boétie. In the first book of these essays, carefully positioned just before its very center, he placed "On Friendship," his paean to La Boétie.

He wanted to imitate the painters of his day, he said at the start of "On Friendship": painters choose a spot on the wall for their picture and then frame it with charming grotesques. Accordingly, Montaigne's essay "On Friendship" would form the frame of a very special centerpiece: a discourse on *Voluntary Servitude*, a call to liberty, written by La Boétie in his youth. That discourse was doubly meaningful because it had been the "medium of our first acquaintance."[19] It was how Montaigne first learned of La Boétie – much as Laelius had first been drawn to Scipio when he heard about the latter's virtue. Since Montaigne's books of essays were all (as he claimed) self-portraits, it would seem that he meant to illustrate in the most concrete way possible La Boétie's position as "another self," by introducing his friend's essay with his own.

Yet Montaigne didn't follow through with the plan. At the very end of "On Friendship," he reversed course, writing that the times were not right to publish La Boétie's incendiary words. (It is true that neither the Church nor the monarchy would have looked upon them kindly.) Instead, he'd substitute some sonnets written by his friend. In the first edition of Montaigne's *Essays*, twenty-nine sonnets by La Boétie were published as the "essay" after "Friendship," in the very middle of Book 1. Later, though, they were taken out, leaving a hole right where the book's focus should have been.

Some scholars think we should not take Montaigne at his word, arguing that he was the author of both *Voluntary Servitude* and the sonnets.[20] That would indeed be the perfect pendant for the fantasy of total accord: Montaigne claiming for his friend what he himself had written, as if authorship didn't matter. But let us assume, with most scholars, that even the wily Montaigne did not wish to go that far. If so, then Montaigne's celebration of his "captured will" submerged into La Boétie's doesn't seem to accord with his friend's argument in *Voluntary Servitude*, which praises the will's freedom.

In a Latin poem dedicated to Montaigne, La Boétie wrote, "Our friendship has already reached a rare degree of perfection. [. . . As in grafting like with like,] so it is with souls."[21] But in *Voluntary Servitude* he stressed the dangers of grafting because it may happen that an unlike branch is joined to a tree, and then the fruit comes out all wrong. Like Cicero, La Boétie worried about deformed friendships, corrupted by false loyalty and allowed to take the wrong turn. True friendship, he argued, is holy, natural, and rational. But if the trust and "growing together" that friends experience with one another is transferred to the public sphere, then it all too easily turns into toadyism on behalf of a tyrant. Montaigne's ideal, where "goods, wives, children, honor, and life" are held in common, then becomes a terrible vice: "to see a countless number of people not obeying but serving; not being governed but tyrannized; with neither property, nor relations, nor wives, nor children, nor even their lives belonging to them." The tyrant is the "other self" as monster: "Where did he get so many eyes to spy on you, if you are not granting them to him? How does he have so many hands to strike you, if he does not get them from you?"[22] In *Voluntary Servitude*, love is readily counterfeited and easily mistaken. You may fool yourself into believing you and another are like-minded when you are really his servile lackey.

If Montaigne had indeed wanted *Voluntary Servitude* to follow "Friendship" in his essay collection, then he may well have done so to temper his story of a perfect relationship with a few well-placed cautions. But, in the end, he substituted some love sonnets. Did they serve the same monitory purpose? Yes: they tell the tale of a poet besotted, under the thumb of a "tyrant" named Love, who whips up the poet's hopes only to snuff them out as he pursues a lady who both encourages and spurns him.[23] Relationships with women were always imperfect. "Friendship" and the writing that was to follow it – whether the discourse on liberty or the poems on love – were not, then, entirely idyllic affirmations of like-mindedness but, rather, tandem explorations of its possibilities and pitfalls.

As for the trap of friendship with women, Montaigne stated flatly that none can be another self: "the ordinary capacity of women does not correspond with the communion and fellowship that nurture this sacred bond."[24] Yet later in life, while preparing a new edition of his essays, he apparently wrote a retraction on a loose sheet inserted in his essay "On Presumption." It named Marie de Gournay as a true friend.

Gournay first read Montaigne's *Essays* in 1584 but met him only in 1588, just four years before his death. Nearly forty years younger than he, she offered him (as the retraction declared) the hope that she "will one day be capable of the finest things and, among others, the perfection of that most sacred friendship, to which we do not read that her sex has been able yet to attain."[25] When Montaigne died, it was Gournay who prepared his essays for a new edition; they came out in 1595 along with the note of retraction, which some scholars think she wrote. The more important point for us is that she herself clung to the ideal of a woman as "another self." In the preface that she wrote for her new edition of his *Essays*, she claimed to have had a friendship with Montaigne comparable to the one he had with La Boétie, declaring that she "alone had the perfect knowledge of that great soul (*ame*)," and boasting that Montaigne considered her mind (*ame*) "similar to his own." "Friendship," she declared, echoing Montaigne, "is a double life: to be a friend is to be [oneself] twice."[26]

Mirroring

For the ancient Greek Aristophanes, the "doubling" of the self was rendered imperative by the gods; for the medieval thinker Aelred, it was the result of Christ's spiritual infusion; for Montaigne, living in the long century of religious wars, it was mediated by "I know not what inexplicable and predestined power."[27] Such explanations were unacceptable to Enlightenment thinkers in the seventeenth and eighteenth centuries. They wanted to function as *scientists* of morality, society, and political life.

This was the brief of Scottish philosopher David Hume (d. 1776) when he came to consider our propensity to resonate with other human beings. Inspired by Newton's discovery of the laws of the physical world, Hume spent his life figuring out the laws of *human* nature. Like other scientists, he did experiments – in his case, thought experiments – and, like them, he dealt with abstractions, postulating a human devoid of individual peculiarities. The Aristotelian laws of motion had been overthrown by Galileo and Newton who, unlike Aristotle, postulated perfectly flat surfaces on which utterly smooth balls would roll forever, even though such balls and surfaces did not exist in real life. Hume's hypothetical "human mind," too, was simplified, reduced to its most essential elements, and abstracted from any particular context.

Just as the law of gravity says that all bodies consisting of mass are attracted to each other, so Hume identified a principle – he called it sympathy – that leads us to feel what others are feeling and thinking, even if their sentiments are far from our own. We know how others feel from their facial expressions, behaviors, postures; we "catch" their feelings and feel them ourselves. When people are far away and very different from us in manners and morals, our sympathy, like gravity in a like situation, is minimal. When, however, we are with people who are very much like us, the effect of sympathy is powerful. And when we are near to people dear to us, we feel their feelings "in the strongest and most lively manner" (2.1.11.6).[28] A good and humane person is capable of the most exquisite sensitivity "to the smallest concerns of his friend." Hume offered himself as an example: "my heart catches the same passion [as my friend], and is warmed by those warm sentiments." These feelings are very pleasant and "must give me an affection to everyone that excites them." When that pleasure is as strong as it is in the case of Hume and his friend, it is "love itself" (3.3.3.5).

In other words, sympathy (which is nothing like sympathy as the term is used today) creates a kind of continuum of like-mindedness. At one end, among people who don't know each other and are not very much alike, it is fairly weak; at the other extreme, among people nearby and similar to us, it is very strong. But it's not as if everyone we know well arouses our love. To the contrary: rather, it's their "virtue, knowledge, wit, good sense, [and] good humor" – and other admirable qualities, such as beauty – that elicits our "love and esteem" (2.2.1.4). The sense that another person is another self at a certain general level is a given.

It is the necessary *backdrop* for love; but it is not love unless the other person has the qualities that are lovable. Love may exist on its own, but, like a radical molecule, it often combines with other feelings. Normally, it is joined with benevolence – that word so important to Cicero. Sometimes it is also compounded with "the bodily appetite for generation" – sex (2.2.11.1). It stands to reason that people brought together by these many feelings are exceedingly like-minded. Hume offered a scientific theory to explain Odysseus' marital blessing.

Today that science continues in studies of "empathy." Originally, the term referred to viewers' tendency to project their own feelings onto works of art, but it was taken over by psychologists and psychiatrists to mean the capacity to feel what others are feeling. In 1991, neuropsychologists in Parma, Italy, discovered "mirror neurons" in monkeys – neurons that fired both when monkeys performed gestures and when they simply *observed* other monkeys making the same movements. Although initially tied only to the mirroring of motor skills, mirror neurons are said by some scientists to be involved in emotional empathy as well. Various studies, reports neuroscientist Marco Iacoboni, show that "mirror neuron areas, the insula, and the amygdala [regions of the brain] were activated for both observation and imitation of facial emotional expressions, with higher activity during imitation."[29] Psychologist Jan Rostowski makes still loftier claims, asserting that mirror neurons "play a very important role, especially in close interpersonal relationships based on love." And, as if he has found the scientific basis for Nestor's like-mindedness with Odysseus, he continues, "[They help assure] perseverance and success in these complex interpersonal relationships, which are indeed responsible for . . . the implementation of joint undertakings."[30]

But, after all, the fantasy of another self is based on the idea of *finding* someone of like mind rather than on a *universal* aptitude to feel what another is feeling. If mirror neurons tingle when we see the intentions and emotions of others, what prevents us from falling in love with almost everyone? Worse, if carried to its logical extreme, the mirror neuron theory of love would suggest that the partner whose neurons fire first would then take on the emotional and intentional coloring of his – or her – beloved. Love's inequalities would be built into human hard wiring.

A pillow shared

Before the mid-nineteenth century, same-sex friendships could be "romantic" yet not dubbed "homosexual," even if sex played a role in them. The seventeenth-century epitaph on the tombstone for John Finch and Thomas Baines read, sentimentally and admiringly: "joined in life; not divided in death."[31] The sort of relationship that Finch and Baines had – half friendship (perhaps erotic), half brotherhood – was fairly common in the United States in the early nineteenth century. In his youth, Daniel Webster (d. 1852) – the eventual U.S. Secretary of State – found in James Hervey Bingham "the only friend of my heart, the partner of my joys, griefs, and affections, the only participant in my most secret thoughts." He had clearly read his Cicero and Montaigne. Some men of his era revealed yet greater intimacy. Albert Dodd described how he and his friend Anthony Halsey often shared a pillow, "and then how sweet to sleep with him, to hold his beloved form in my embrace, to have his arms about my neck, to imprint upon his face sweet kisses!" He was unembarrassed; this was not a "queer" relationship but, to the contrary, a normal one for men of his class. It blended seamlessly, on the one hand, with their childhood experiences (since often brothers shared one bed) and, on the other, with what we might call "puppy love" for a girl or young woman. It was very typical of such men to tell their "bosom pal" about the women they fancied even as they imagined how idyllic it would be (as Webster wrote to his friend) "to yoke together again; your little bed is just wide enough, we will practice at the same bar and be as friendly a pair of single fellows as ever cracked a nut."[32]

Webster never crossed "the line between the great ideal of friendship and the whisper of suggested sodomy."[33] For him, that frontier was genital sexuality, and in some emotional communities today it remains a deadly one. In the novel (and movie) *Brokeback Mountain*, two young men accustomed to hardscrabble lives meet during a stint herding sheep one long summer. They talk, share meals, are "respectful of each other's opinions, each glad to have a companion where none had been expected."[34] Gradually they become (as the premodern theorists would have put it) one soul in two bodies, and soon more than that: "They never talked about the sex, let it happen." The silence made it acceptable. "I'm not no queer," said one; "Me neither," said the other. They were together, on and off, for life – until one was bludgeoned to death. They called each other "friend." Forgetting labels, we may say that they loved each other. They were "two in one." Nevertheless, they both married, had children.

As did Webster. The difference is that Webster gave up, and apparently without regret, his passionate same-sex friendships, as did most of his male peers. Indeed, Webster probably expected this to happen for, even as he longed to share his life with Bingham, he also found their fond conversation to be "almost childish."[35]

Giving up a "childish" friendship was not the case, however, for women living in Webster's day. Consider Sarah Butler Wister and Jeannie Field Musgrove, who met as teenagers and remained close thereafter. When circumstances forced them apart, they wrote passionate letters to each other: "I shall be entirely alone [this coming week]," wrote Sarah, "I can give you no idea how desperately I shall want you." A letter written by Jeannie began, "Dear darling Sarah! How I love you & how happy I have been! You are the joy of my life." Each expected the other to wish her all the best at all times, but they sometimes needed reassurances. As Jeannie wrote, "I want you to tell me in your next letter, to assure me, that I am your dearest. . . . I long to hear you say it once more. . . . So just fill a quarter page with caresses & expressions of endearment."[36] Historian Carroll Smith-Rosenberg studied many women like Sarah and Jeannie. Although they had in common their middle-class origins, they represented diverse backgrounds and geographical regions. Almost all eventually became wives and mothers, but they nevertheless turned to other women for both practical and emotional support, passing smoothly from the domesticity of their childhood homes to that of their married households. They did not give up their intense friendships in adulthood.

But in the twenty-first century the desire for autonomy could outweigh the joy of finding a "second self." In the Neapolitan novels of Elena Ferrante, Lenù and Lila are childhood girlfriends in an impoverished neighborhood in the 1950s and remain friends well into adulthood. Narrated by Lenù, now in her sixties, the story begins with a series of childish dares, Lila doing something dangerous first, Lenù, her "heart pounding," following suit. But, once Lila took Lenù's hand on the scariest of their adventures, "this gesture changed everything between us forever."[37] The two became inseparable and yet antagonistic, vying with each other in ways small and large. Lila humiliated Lenù with her brilliance and audacity; Lenù admired Lila and strove to catch up. Both girls loved and hated each other at the same time. When the two were adults Lila entrusted Lenù with a box of her personal papers. Lenù read them (though strictly charged not to do so), memorized some passages, and admired them even while "feeling deceived." At last, she "couldn't stand feeling Lila on me and in me" and threw the box into the Arno river. There was indeed a mingling of two souls here, but for the narrator it was intolerable.

*

In *Enlightened*, Amy Jellicoe imagined that she and Sandy were best friends. "A friend," she says in voice-over, is "someone who really gets you, who sees you, every side of you, someone who can even reveal yourself to you. . . . You have found your kind." This is the fantasy of the other self. When Amy and Sandy meet at the airport, they hug tightly, their arms and legs dancing together like the Aristophanic vision of the original human being. Yet, by the end of the episode, Amy admits to Sandy: "You barely know me. . . . There are things you'll never know about me, just as there are things I'll never know about you."

In Homer, the idea of like-mindedness was connected to joint enterprises: military strategy, running a household. Like two musicians in a duet, friends and spouses played their separate parts, yet the result was harmony. In Plato, the issue of power was so clear that he preferred to present perfect merging as a myth. But with Aristotle it went back to being a practical matter, albeit rare and wonderful: friends were other selves above all because together they developed their capacities as rational beings – Aristotle's definition of virtue.

And that set the terms of finding "another self" until the time of Montaigne, though the idea of virtue was soon Christianized. Then, too, someone like Heloise had her own very personal take on the consequences of "likeness in character and concerns." But when, in the writings of Hume and later, the Christian definition of virtue fell out of the picture for many, then the fantasy of "another self" had to find new moorings. Mirror neurons seemed (and seem) to make like-mindedness a fact of nature. At last, women meet men on equal ground. Taken to an extreme, mirroring would seem to be totalizing, meaning that everything – one's actions, intentions, goals, and emotions – will be felt by the other. But what then happens to the "self" of that other? Even Montaigne, who rejoiced in being "one soul in two bodies" with La Boétie, had doubts, which he expressed in the guise of his friend's writings.

In any case, mirror neurons are only part of our psychology, and, as willful human beings, we often refuse to follow even the seemingly scientific laws of brain circuitry. A taxi-driver in Afghanistan who lost his legs to a bomb reports that many people mock him: they don't feel the loss of their own legs (even if perchance their neurons fire when they see him) but, to the contrary, feel like pointing a finger in derision.[38] In *Enlightened*, Amy is soon only pretending to be on the same page with Sandy; by the end, she acknowledges the charade.

The Aristophanic myth hangs on today, not least in the occultist-inflected guise of "twin flames" – the belief that, "back in the time when the universe was created, each of us had a twin flame with whom we shared a single force of energy."[39] The fantasy of like-mindedness has been uprooted from its originally limited sense of harmonious agreement in common enterprises. Briefly offered by Plato as an egalitarian ideal uniting citizens of all genders, it was soon turned (largely) into the prerogative of an "old boys' club" within Roman and Christian circles. Universalized as "sympathy" by Hume and as empathy by some scientists, it persists today. Given its history, we may wish to give it a second look. What sort of like-mindedness do we mean or want?

2

Transcendence

Number one on the Billboard Rhythm & Blues chart in 1967, Jackie Wilson's "(Your Love Keeps Lifting Me) Higher and Higher" expresses love's uplifting power. Higher and higher: as he sings the words, Wilson's voice rises to a stratospheric falsetto; his normal human tenor simply will not do.[1]

But why higher? Why doesn't love ground us, root us?

This is what I call the "transcendent fantasy" of love – the idea that "true love" lifts us above the quotidian. We see it in Marc Chagall's *The Birthday* (1915), where two lovers (in fact, Chagall and his fiancée, Bella) rise over the red floor of a humble apartment, kissing in rapture (see figure 3). Later, Bella, now married to the painter, described the glorious moment: "You soared up to the ceiling. . . . Then together we floated up above the room with all its finery, and flew. Through the window a cloud and a patch of blue sky called to us. The brightly hung walls whirled around us. We flew over fields of flowers, shuttered houses, roofs, yards, churches."[2]

Beyond the body

Love transcends; love lifts us above the mundane. A modest room becomes the setting for a pair of passionate lovers to leap beyond its confines.

Yet in Plato's *Symposium*, in which the philosopher shows how and why love does this, the sort of transcendence that Wilson and Chagall celebrate is belittled. It's just the starting point for something far better and higher. And on that point, love beyond *human* love, rests the weight of Western thought and tradition.

To be precise, in the *Symposium* Plato doesn't speak. Nor does his hero Socrates take center stage. Rather, Socrates presents himself as the mouthpiece of the priestess Diotima, who (Socrates declares) instructed him on this matter so complex and difficult that she was not sure even he could understand it. Diotima denies that love (*Eros*) is a god (as all the other speakers have asserted); he is, rather, a daemon, a spirit, a sort of middleman between humans and the gods. Love's mother was the daemon Need – always seeking something – while his father was the daemon Resourcefulness. So love, like his mother, always strives to have what he needs – including wisdom, beauty, the "good" – and always, like his father, he finds clever ways to get it. When people "are in love," that really means that they are inspired by *Eros* to want "to possess the good forever" (206a).[3] They manage this in the only way possible for mortals. They "give birth" to the good that they desire. Love's purpose, says Diotima, is "giving birth in beauty, whether in body or in soul" (206b). Plato's word for beauty here, *kalon*, covered all that was good both physically and ethically. Love alone gives humans the possibility of having "the good *forever*." Children are "what mortals have in place of immortality" (207a).

Then Diotima moves on. She doesn't mean what people ordinarily mean by "children." She says that everyone is pregnant – that is, everyone is about to give birth to something – but to give life to the future child that they hold latently, as it were, they must love. Men pregnant "in body" will love a woman and produce a boy or a girl. But, continues Diotima, that is not the best way to achieve an afterlife that will go on forever. Children may sicken and die. Even if they live, they may not themselves produce more children.

This seems a very odd thing for a woman to say. The woman's domain in ancient Greece was the household, and her main role was the production of children. But this fictive woman is not ordinary: she is a priestess and, as such, was obliged to abstain from sex and, therefore, from physical procreation. It stands to reason, then, that she has a solution better than giving birth to mortal children. For (she says) some children are born of the soul. Those pregnant in their souls rather than in their bodies will seek "a soul that is beautiful and noble and well-formed," someone who will make them "instantly teem with ideas and arguments about virtue" (209b–c). Diotima seems to have in mind the Athenian lover responsible for the moral formation of his young beloved. "Ideas and arguments about virtue" are better than giving birth to boys and girls because ideas are nearly deathless. Yet even they have weaknesses, for (as Plato demonstrates constantly in his dialogues) ideas and arguments almost always go astray or remain incomplete.

Thus, lovers will not stop with a beautiful soul, which, after all, belongs to just another person. They will realize that they must follow an upward path, a "ladder of love." To be sure, they must step on the first rung, love for a beautiful body. But they will soon move on to the next, for every beautiful body is like another. Plato is denying the importance of individual differences even in nature and character. Adopting that perspective is like looking down at human beings from the moon. It is precisely what Plato means to do.

For lovers must mount higher, far beyond embodied beauty, where they will find laws and knowledge and all the things that are morally valuable. The ladder's rungs (from bodies to souls to laws to ideas) represent love's right order, but all must be left behind if lovers are to reach their final goal: the sight "of something wonderfully beautiful in its nature." This something "always *is* and neither comes to be nor passes away.... It is not anywhere in another thing, as in an animal, or in earth, or in heaven, or in anything else, but [is] itself by itself with itself" (211a–b). At last lovers are "with" (here Plato uses a term that was also used for intercourse) their ultimate beloved, and "with" it they give birth "to true virtue" (212a). Love thus leads from a human being – including all his (or her) flaws and passing beauty and the certainty of death – to the "beautiful itself, absolute, pure, unmixed, not polluted by human flesh or colors or any other great nonsense of mortality" (211e). If anyone can be immortal, concludes Diotima, it is the lover who has followed love to these heights.

How can Diotima speak of "the nonsense of mortality"? These are such strong words. They batter against the normal assumptions of the ancient world, where infant death was an implacable fact of life and where, therefore, all were expected to wed and contribute to the population. Having mortal children was a singular and highly regarded achievement. To be sure, a man was expected to exercise self-control and not engage overmuch in sexual intercourse. Too much sex would, the doctors said, deplete his vital spirit. But no man should reject the nuptial bed. Reproduction was essential, whether or not it was accompanied by erotic thrill.

*

The reproductive imperative remained true nearly a millennium after Plato's day, when the Roman Empire wrapped itself around the Mediterranean Sea and spread its tentacles in all directions. There, as in ancient Greece, marriage and procreation were considered essential social obligations. Marriages, though generally contracted for unsentimental reasons, were supposed to be stable, happy, harmonious, peaceful – and, yes, loving. Here is how the poet Lucretius described the words of mourners as they gathered to recall a family man recently deceased:

> "Never again," mourners say, "will your household receive you with joy; never again will the best of wives welcome you home; never again will your dear children race for the prize of your first kisses and touch your heart with pleasure too profound for words."[4]

These must have been typical sentiments and therefore ripe for Lucretius' Epicurean mocking. A dead man, he pointed out, can feel nothing at all.

Christianity, which by the third century had made significant inroads into this society, did not so much turn these ancient values upside down as subordinate them to a higher and utterly transcendent love, though not the one promised by Diotima. Indeed, in effect, Christ took the place of Diotima's *Eros*, for, in much of Christian thought, it was Christ who mediated the lover's ascent to immortality.

Initially, in the context of sporadic persecutions, a number of Christians saw martyrdom as the way to walk in Christ's footsteps and achieve eternal life. Martyrdom's transcendent possibilities were made clear in the example of Saint Perpetua. Around the year 200, as a young mother and recent Christian convert caught in the maw of imperial power, she wrote of her experiences while awaiting execution. Her father came to her in prison, trying desperately to persuade her to recant: "Think about your brothers, think about your mother and your mother's sister, think about your son [an infant at the breast] who will not be able to live without you."[5] But Perpetua's eyes were fixed on heaven. Indeed, she had her own vision of a ladder, though hers (unlike Diotima's) was narrow and lined with sharp "swords, lances, hooks, knives, and daggers, so that if anyone climbed up carelessly, or [was] not looking upwards, he was torn to pieces and his flesh clung to the iron weapons." Perpetua "looked upwards," indeed, and climbed "in the name of Jesus Christ." At the top (she reported) she saw "an enormous garden and a white-haired man . . . dressed in shepherd's clothes, a big man, milking sheep." This was Christ, whose white hair echoed Revelation 1:13–14, "I saw one like the Son of Man. . . . His head and his hair were white as white wool, white as snow." He gave her some delicious cheese to eat, while thousands of white-clad people welcomed her. Soon after this vision, "as God willed," Perpetua recorded that her child no longer needed to nurse; she could leave it behind.

Jacob's ladder on which angels "were ascending and descending" (Genesis 28:12) and Diotima's ladder of love merged in Perpetua's vision. New with Perpetua was the wrenching emotional suffering that the ascent entailed. The result made for a treacherous but ultimately ecstatic climb. Jacob's ladder had required no exertion, for the angels moved up and down effortlessly. Rather similarly, Diotima's hypothetical ladder-climbing lover unproblematically left the original "beautiful body" behind along with all the other phantoms of earthly existence. Perpetua's ascent was less insouciant. The cutting implements on the ladder symbolized her bodily and psychic pain even as she looked ever upward.

Perpetua understood herself to be transcending not only her family and her motherhood (so key to the very identity of the Roman matron) but also her gender: in a vision she saw herself in the arena where the wild beasts were to tear her apart, "and I was stripped naked, and I became a man." As a man, she had to wrestle with "a

certain Egyptian, foul in appearance." After she bested
her opponent, she was welcomed by the Roman throng
as the victor, "and I began to walk in triumph to the
Gate of Life." Then she woke up. But the anonymous
contemporary who incorporated her "diary" into his
account of her martyrdom must have been uncomfortable with her allusion to a gender transformation, for he
reported that, when the day of her martyrdom dawned
and all the prisoners marched joyously to the amphi-
theater, "Perpetua followed, with a shining face and a
calm step, as a wife of Christ and darling of God."

A generation later, as Christianity began to seep
into the very corners of the empire and persecutions
were coming to an end, a new sort of martyrdom
was adumbrated: virginity. Even in the context of
early Christianity, this was something of an anomaly.
Christianity could never entirely deny the material
world and the human body because it was rooted in
the idea of a divinity made flesh, in a Lord who cared
enough about a human wedding to turn water into wine
and who told his disciplines that the bread and wine on
a dinner table was his body and blood. But Christ also
suffered on the cross, and, gradually, physical self-denial
came to be seen (by influential clerics and those who
listened to them, at least) as the best way to live out the
Christian life. The priest and biblical exegete Origen
(d. 253), knew Plato's *Symposium* well and was himself a Platonist. But he ridiculed its discussion of *Eros*,
which (as he pointed out) took place amid mouthfuls
of food and gulps of wine. In his commentary on the
biblical Song of Songs, Origen separated carnal from
spiritual love, skipping the first rung of Diotima's ladder
entirely. The "inner man," he whose soul did not live in
this world despite the grounding of his body, was led by
love "from earth to the lofty heights of heaven." [6] The
inner man was not the sort to "rush into carnal sins and
down the steep places of immodesty." For Origen and

many others, virginity was coming to be understood as the knot that tied heaven to earth. Diotima's first rung, the love of a beautiful body, was for these Christians worse than a mistake: "If you are a lover of the flesh, you do not acquire the love of the spirit." There was no chance a Christian like Origen would float over a city in an ecstatic kiss with another human being. Little wonder that he interpreted the Song spiritually: just as Jewish exegetes understood it as a dialogue between God and Israel, so Origen made it the love duet of Christ and his Church, of the Word and the human soul.

The Roman Empire became officially Christian at the end of the fourth century, and the self-sacrifice of martyrs became moot. But the impulse to follow in Christ's painful footsteps led to new religious movements of prayer and privation. First came the hermits (who lived alone, or nearly so) and then the monks (who lived together in communities). Monasteries were governed by various rules and customs; the Rule of Saint Benedict, widely adopted in the West after c.800, provided a skeletal framework that each monastic house interpreted to suit its needs, preoccupations, and desires. Given the overriding prestige and power of monasteries in medieval Europe, the Rule might almost serve as a touchstone for its civilization as a whole. That's why it matters that, although the transcendent possibilities of love were not very visible in this Rule, they nevertheless existed. We find them under the unexpected rubric of "humility," inspired by the scriptural assertion (turning common sense on its head) that "everyone who exalts himself will be humbled, and he who humbles himself will be exalted" (Luke 18:14). "So, brothers," wrote Benedict, "if we want to . . . arrive quickly at that heavenly exaltation toward which we ascend through humility in this present life, . . . we must raise the ladder that appeared to Jacob in his dream" (7.5–6).[7] Monks and nuns climbed this ladder by progressively denying their own will – substituting in its place obedience to the Rule, to the abbot (the monastic superior), and to God. In Benedict's hands the emotion driving this ascent was (at first) not love but, rather, fear. In the Christian vision, mankind turned away from loving God when Adam and Eve fell from Paradise. The monks and nuns making their ascent had therefore first to fear God's wrath. As they made their way up the rungs, however, fear would be joined by other feelings – suffering, hope, guilt, low self-esteem – until, at last, at the top, they would reach "God's loving-kindness that 'once perfected drives out fear'" (1 John 4:18). Now all the obedience initially performed out of fear was practiced "without any effort and as if naturally by habit, no longer in the fear of hell, but instead in the love of Christ" (7.67–9). The monk was expected to make an emotional transformation.

Divine love

In the Rule of Benedict, the "love of Christ" was set in opposition to erotic love. The Cistercians – Benedictine monks, but a distinct order that flourished in the twelfth century and later – were among the first to infuse religious love with the pungent fluids and fierce heat of the flesh. They made the ascent to God an erotic experience. This was no doubt tied to the Cistercians' rejection of the hitherto widespread practice of "oblation," when parents offered their children to the monastic life. Cistercians, by contrast, entered the many monasteries of their order as mature men, seasoned in the ways of the world and its erotic temptations and possibilities. They knew the feelings and the literatures of sexual desire, burning passion, and obsessive love that is the topic of chapter 4.

When the Cistercian abbot Saint Bernard (d. 1153), one of the most influential figures of his century, expounded on the biblical Song of Songs, he used it to celebrate the joys and sensual pleasures of the world beyond this one. Taking as his starting point the idea that the Song celebrated the love between God and the soul, he endowed the soul with the emotional sensibilities of the body, desirous and yearning.

Motivated at first (as in the Rule) by fear, the stalled soul's ignition key, the soul overcomes its misguided love of self and the world. It longs for the promise of the first line of the Song: "Let him kiss me with the kiss of his mouth!" (Song 1:2.)[8] Not so fast, chides Bernard. Though you are the "bride" of the Song, you are just starting out and cannot yet aspire so high. Diotima's ladder had demanded a succession of epiphanies about the nature of beauty; Perpetua's ladder was so beset with dangers that it required total focus on the goal; Bernard's ascent, by contrast to both, and in keeping with the Benedictine Rule, requires self-mortification. You have to begin literally at the bottom, preparing yourself for the Bridegroom's kiss with bitter weeping, deep sighing, and sobs of repentance. Then "prostrate yourself on the ground, take hold of [Christ's] feet, soothe them with kisses, sprinkle them with your tears, and so wash not them but yourself. . . . But even then, you may not dare to lift up a face suffused with shame and grief, until you hear the sentence: 'Your sins are forgiven'" (Luke 7:48) (1.17). Still, there is more to do: you must continue to climb with good deeds, and so (not yet ready for the kiss of the mouth) you may kiss Christ's hand. At last you are ready for "unbounded joy": the kiss of the mouth – the moment when the Lord reveals himself to the soul (1.20).

The pursuit of transcendence is thus not for the feeble of heart. But it results in blissful fecundity. For the "kiss of the mouth" is so potent that, "no sooner has the bride received it than she conceives, and her breasts grow rounded with the fruitfulness of conception."

Bernard reminds his fellow monks that they have had this experience from time to time: spiritually parched and thirsty as they approach the altar, they feel the infusion of God's grace watering their "dry and lukewarm" hearts. The "milk of sweet fecundity" that gushes forth from them is much more wonderful – and far more lasting – than the pale pleasures of "sensual passions," all of which inevitably end with death (1.58, 60).

Even so, the kiss, the conception, and the swollen breasts are but preludes to the final goal, for the Bridegroom now draws the soul into his bedroom. Bernard himself has "sometimes gained happy entrance. Alas! how rare the time, and how short the stay!" (2.38). Only in heaven will such delights be eternal.

The Song of Songs – with its evocation of fragrant oils, clusters of blossoms, sweet tastes – is frankly sensual, and Bernard happily expands on its erotic imagery because, as he explains, only thus can the lover of God be enticed away from the shallow but potent pleasures of the world. Bernard's ascent prescribes a sort of homeopathy; the erotics of God ward off those of the bed. In Diotima's scheme the soul rose to unite with absolute beauty, leaving behind all the pollution of the mortal world. In Bernard's, even the perfumes of the world are harnessed to arrive at the Lord's bedchamber.

*

Medieval mystics like Bernard were legion among the educated male elite and influential among the less well read. So, too, were female mystics, and none more so than the poet Marguerite Porete. "Love draws me so high," she wrote, sounding a bit like Jackie Wilson. But Wilson was talking about his feelings for a very special girl, while Marguerite was writing about her emptiness and lack of feelings. As Lady Love "with her divine gaze" draws her up, she celebrates her loss of thought and will.[9] The soul, she says, makes the ascent to God through the annihilation of self, so that it becomes nothing other than God. "God is love," declares 1 John 4:8. "I am nothing except Love," says the Soul in Marguerite's *Mirror of Simple Souls*.

Probably well born and certainly very well read, Porete was a beguine – unmarried and chaste but not a nun – existing on the margins of established institutions, practicing an intensely devout life that ended when she was convicted of heresy and burned at the stake in 1310. Her book, originally written in French, was copied and circulated within pious circles and translated into Latin, English, and Italian. Yet it was but one rivulet in the medieval poetic outpouring about love, both human and divine, that we shall explore further with Dante in this chapter and again in chapter 4. Drawing on learned Neoplatonic philosophical theology, popular romances, and theatrical performances, Porete delivers her ideas via an animated, chaotic, and occasionally ecstatic dialogue among Lady Love, the Simple Soul, Reason, and other personifications.

In the beginning, before the Fall, says the *Mirror*, there was nothing but God, and the soul willed nothing but what God willed. But now, for the most part, the soul is "less than nothing," and it becomes ever smaller whenever it wills something on its own. Yet there is a way – an ascent of seven stages – in which the soul may recover its original nothingness and become "nothing except Love." Ordinary people have salvation; Christ and his Church (with its sacraments, prayers, and good works) ensure that. But the souls of "those who are dead to the life of the spirit and live the divine life" experience something unspeakably more glorious: "the flower from the boiling of love. . . . This love of which we speak is the union of lovers, the inflaming fire which burns without consuming."

As for Perpetua, so for Porete: the ascent is daunting and the arrival unutterably wonderful. The process begins (on the first rung) with souls already well advanced because they practice good works and yet know "that there is a being better than theirs." They begin "miserable and sad," and some fall by the wayside, for "a petty heart dares not to undertake a great thing or to climb high, because of a lack of love." Their climb demands (at the second rung) self-mortification and sacrifice and worse: for while in the course of its ascent the soul delights in all the "works of goodness" that it has been doing, it must now (on the third level) abstain from them in order to further deny the self. Danger awaits the soul at stage four, for from this high vantage point the soul may indeed contemplate its beloved and imagine that its journey has ended. In that, it is wrong; it is still subject to its own will, "proud of the abundance of love" and dazzled by its success. It must recognize (this is the fifth stage) that it is nothing at all until "the Divine Goodness pours out from [His] bosom one rapturous overflow of the movement of Divine Light." The soul then dissolves and becomes one with God.

This would seem to be the culmination of the ascent, and yet there is something more: momentary glimpses of God, as if through "an aperture, like a spark, which quickly closes." In this, the sixth stage, God sees himself in the soul but the soul does not see itself, for it no longer has a self (see figure 4). In the seventh stage, which will be the happy fate of the emptied soul forever once it leaves the body, it "swims and flows in joy, without feeling any joy, for [it] dwells in Joy and Joy dwells in [it]." Never in Plato, never in the Rule, never even in the Lord's bedchamber was there so complete an erasure of the separate human soul in love's union.

*

But let us return to earth, where we find the young Dante Alighieri (d. 1321) glimpsing the equally young Beatrice on the streets of Florence and saying to himself,

"Now has appeared your beatitude."[10] From that day on, he insisted later, "Love ruled over my soul." "Love ruled," as if it came from outside and entered his soul through that single glimpse at an unguarded moment. Such an idea was traditional and continues today with the commonplace saying "love at first sight." It explains why figures of Love shoot arrows in numerous depictions, as shown in figure 5, a betrothal casket. In medieval optical theory, the eyes send out rays to "grasp" their object and/or they *receive* rays from the object. Before Love could rule Dante, he had to see the object of his love.

He was nine years old "when to my eyes first appeared the glorious lady of my mind." "Of his mind" in part because, when he wrote those words in his *New Life*, a brilliantly original mélange of self-exploration, poetry, and philosophy composed in the early 1290s, Beatrice had been dead for a few years. In part, too, because she really was largely "of his mind," the creation of an artist determined to make her the leitmotif of his life. For Dante, Beatrice functioned somewhat like Diotima's daemon *Eros* – inspiring both his neediness and his craftiness, especially the craft of writing his exceptional poetry, his own immortal children.

Beatrice was very much a real person. She married into an illustrious family around the age of eighteen and died in her twenties. (Dante's own marriage, a few years after hers, was at a lower social level.) Yet, as he described her in the *New Life*, she both was and was not of this world. When he first saw her (she was eight years old), she was wearing crimson red, a reminder of Christ and the blood he shed on the Cross. In the next encounter, precisely nine years later, she was wearing white, the color of the heavenly host. In the number nine, three times three, Dante understood the Trinity. At that later meeting, Beatrice greeted him "such that I then seemed to see all the terms of beatitude." He dated his "new life" from that moment – the beginning of his sentimental education.

Beatrice's greeting, a "salutation," was equally a "salvation" (both words derive from the Latin *salus*). Overcome "like one inebriated," Dante retired to his room. There he dreamt that Love himself appeared, "joyous" and holding Dante's burning heart in his hand. In Love's arms was "my lady wrapped in a cloth asleep." But then Love

> ... wakened her, and this burning heart
> to the frightened one he humbly fed:
> afterward I saw him turn away weeping.

"My lady" was Beatrice. In its emphasis on love in the here and now, the poem was very much in the literary tradition of his day, and Dante was pleased enough with it to send it to many other love poets. It was a way for him to make himself known to them and to receive their comments. The dream and the sonnet that records it in his *New Life* come at the very start of Dante's ascent through love. At this point, everything is centered on Dante, whose heart is fed to Beatrice much as Christ's body was consumed by the faithful in the Eucharist. Unlike Christ's body, however, Beatrice alone tastes Dante's heart. That is the first and lowest rung of love's ladder, when Dante selfishly keeps Beatrice for himself.

In the next step, however, Dante recognizes that Beatrice's virtues extend to all. They are made better simply by being in her presence: "Many said, after she had passed: 'She is no earthly woman, but one of those most beautiful angels of heaven.'" Now Beatrice is Christ's avatar. She should remind us of Christ as he was understood by Dante's contemporary Saint Francis (d. 1226) – as a heavenly being who pours out His love alike on lepers and the poor, friends and foes, robbers and thieves.

In the *Divine Comedy* (*Commedia*), which Dante started to write perhaps thirteen or so years after finishing the *New Life*, his ascent is complete. It, too, takes place through the mediation of Beatrice, who, "moved by love," comes down from heaven to summon the ancient Roman poet Virgil to save Dante from the dangerous moral path he is following and to show him the horrors that await sinners in Hell and the penance that even the saved must do in Purgatory.[11]

Whenever Dante becomes discouraged during this arduous trip from hell to heaven, the name of Beatrice is enough to urge him on. Finally, having plunged into the depths of deadly hell and clambered up the craggy mountain of Purgatory, he sees her. She arrives – like the coming of Christ – with the dawn. Dante is as overcome as he once was as a boy: "Not a drop of blood is left in me that does not tremble: I know the tokens of the ancient flame." But now she comes as a judge, sharp-tongued and disapproving: after she died, she tells him reproachfully, even though she became thereafter more beautiful and more virtuous, Dante fell out of love with her a bit, "and he turned his steps along a way not true."[12] Grief and contrition overcome Dante, and Beatrice dips him into the river that divides Purgatory from Paradise, giving him a second baptism. Up he goes with her (leaving Virgil behind), through the nine spheres of heaven. In the process, Dante is transformed, "passing beyond humanity" and becoming Godlike.[13] At the final rung Dante sees "the Infinite Goodness" that gathers all into itself.[14]

Plato's final rung had been like this: it too revealed all the beautiful things of the universe in one eternal form. The final moment for Bernard and Porete, too, offered the image of union – in Bernard's case involving all the senses, in Porete's reveling in the loss of self in order to participate in God's own being. But Dante's ladder was different from all the others in the fact that, from first to last, its rungs were defined by his love of Beatrice, a real woman. He could not think of leaving her behind, however spiritualized his love for her became. He never imagined (unlike Plato's Diotima) that the beauty of one Beatrice was a lot like the beauty of another. Nor did he start his ascent already fully committed to the rejection of profane love, as Bernard and Porete had done. Dante's profane love was a *necessary* precondition for him to mount higher and higher. If he went yet higher (at least some would say so) than Jackie Wilson, that does not negate the fact that Dante, too, found transcendence in the love of "one in a million girls."

It says a lot about the influence of Dante that modern Italian owes much to the language in which he wrote.

Transcendence through child-rearing

Recall that Diotima said that love's purpose is "giving birth in beauty," and people may do so "in body" as well as "in soul." She denigrated the first option. She taught Socrates that true, imperishable immortality was to be found only in a kind of absorption in the perfect "form" of beauty, where the gods dwell. Ancient and medieval traditions of love's transcendent potential inherited that vision. These traditions help us see the complex origins of the idea of love's "lift."

But that idea was meant for an elite. Plato was writing for the philosophers at his Academy, Perpetua for a small cadre of early Christians. Monks constituted the primary audience of Benedict and Bernard. Porete wrote for "simple souls" – recall how dismissive she was of "ordinary people" who had "only" salvation to look forward to. Only Dante wrote (he hoped) for a general audience, but his experience, dependent on his love of Beatrice, was his alone. Equally to the point, all these ascents were long and arduous. Few could keep their eyes on the goal, their feet negotiating the many rungs of the ladder.

The Protestant Reformation, which began in the six-teenth century, changed neither the conviction that the human soul was immortal nor that belief in God was necessary for salvation. But it did deny the possibility that a ladder of love could lead a man or a woman to God. People were too mired in the quicksand of sin to mount on their own. Faith alone could pull them up, and faith was a gift from God, who reached down, as it were, to choose those whom he would save. In effect, Luther's revolution turned the Platonic ascent on its head: utterly dependent on God for our loves, we *descend* from Christ's love back to earth, to love others.

Love's direction, then, is upward only after it has come down, from God. Thereafter God's love is encour-aged and strengthened within church congregations and (above all) lived out in families. The high value that Origen, nuns, monks, and so many others placed on vir-ginity in the millennium before the Reformation became moot. In Protestant regions, monasteries and nunner-ies were dissolved. The clergy, monks, and nuns, like everyone else, were to marry. And they were expected to have children, who, if properly brought up, would serve as the legacy of God's love given to them by their parents. From Martin Luther's "Table Talk," a record of his and other ministers' informal comments, comes this: "The love of parents resembles and is an image of the Divine that is impressed upon the human heart. God's love for the human race is as great as the love of parents for their children, as the Scripture says; it is truly great and hot."[15]

The new emphasis on the family as the chief node of God's love within the world led to a proliferation of marital advice books and child-rearing manuals. English divine Richard Baxter (d. 1691) spoke of parental love as the first "motive for a holy and careful education of children." Children, he said, were a veritable limb of the parental tree, their physical and spiritual well-being to be tended carefully: "if you love them, show it in those things on which their everlasting welfare doth depend. Do not say you love them, and yet lead them unto hell."[16] To English minister Isaac Ambrose (d. 1664), the proper raising of children offered salvation to both parents and their progeny. Well-trained children will do the same for their own offspring, and so it will continue until the end of time. Then, on the final day, woe to the parents who had been negligent, for "the rich man will rise up against you on the day of judgment and condemn you."[17]

Even as the importance of the afterlife receded in many circles, religious appeals continued. *Mother's Magazine*, published in the United States in the mid-nineteenth century, infused advice to parents with religious piety. Consider, wrote one mother, that "the law of nature is love. Every mother may remember the emotions with which she first looked upon the face of her child. . . . We once thought of dying for ourselves alone, and we thought to gather the robes of salvation around us and pass into the great spiritual presence without a care. But, my dear friends, we cannot do so now."[18] In other words, once a woman had children, her life and her salvation were bound up with theirs.

But salvation did not have to be invoked to keep the focus on the family and the transcendent possibilities of parenting. There was no ladder for fathers and mothers to climb but, rather, the slow and patient molding of another human being through all the stages of infancy, childhood, youth, and into adulthood. In the eighteenth and nineteenth centuries, the deaths of the parents were envisioned as one more stage of a transcendent process: they were succeeded by their children, who would transmit the self-same virtues to the next generation, and so on. That, at any rate, was the seductive fantasy. Loving and devoted mothers created grateful children ready to carry on the tradition, like the appreciative writer of the poem "My Mother" (1815):

> When pain and sickness made me cry,
> Who gaz'd upon my heavy eye,
> And wept, for fear that I should die?
> My Mother.[19]

Which was soon matched by "My Father" (1817):

> When from my Mother's lap put down,
> I first essayed to walk alone,
> Whose sheltering arms were open thrown?
> My Father's.[20]

Yet death stalked the dreams of these parents and children, as Diotima had darkly warned. When Thomas Wright (d. 1801), a minor government official in England, lost the light of his life, his son John, he recalled the happy days when the child romped and prattled and kissed him, and then the terrible moment when the child died in his arms. Consoling himself, he considered that his loss might have had a heavenly purpose:

> Wast thou withdrawn, my dearest love,
> To urge thy father's rise;
> To draw my heart to things above,
> And call me to the skies[?][21]

Similarly haunted by the ghosts of her dead offspring, Hannah Robertson, writing in the 1770s, lamented "having buried nine children, besides grandchildren."[22]

Both Wright and Robertson wrote autobiographies, full of Dickensian hardships and human perfidy, for their children and succeeding generations, in whom, as Robertson put it, "we again live." Her tale was particularly maudlin: a self-proclaimed granddaughter of the English Restoration King Charles II, she sank in economic well-being over the course of her life, describing herself at the end as an aged grandmother with a "broken heart" caring for an orphaned grandchild. Her only hope, she said, was to be taken under the wing of a noble lady and, when she died, to remain a spirit on "the earth unseen" to watch over her infant charge. Diotima had rejected immortality through children because they might die, but belief in the immortality of the soul negated that objection; even the death of a child would not impede love's transcendent possibilities.

*

These days, argues philosopher Simon May, "the child is becoming the supreme object of love."[23] But, he says, this is precisely *not* because having children offers us a transcendent experience. He redefines love as the joy that comes from finding someone or something that roots and grounds us, in whom we see our "home," however far it may be from where we began. Love's potential is the *opposite* of transcendence for May; it burrows down, takes root, gains nourishment from the soil of whatever world the lover values – whether that is the world in which our feet are planted or another to which we hope to go. In either case, we experience that world, that home, as the source of our very being. Having children nowadays, he says, is for many the first stage of a journey to an unknown but ever so promising place, even though the trip will never come to a perfect conclusion. For May the fantasy is to experience a *complete* sense of rootedness.

May puts the emphasis on us – our needs and our desires to feel "at home." Similarly focused on the self is the argument of Harry Frankfurt, another philosopher writing today. Love, he says, is caring about what is important to ourselves. When we are committed to ourselves (as most of us are), then we love those things that matter to us and to our life's goals. We need to love, and out of that comes our "disinterested concern" in the well-being of those whom we love.[24] This is easiest to see when it comes to ourselves (Frankfurt is happy with the idea of self-love) and our children, both of whom we love out of a biological imperative "embedded in our nature." Frankfurt's love is not transcendent because it always comes back to the self. It is a "configuration of the will" – of *our* will, which is the product of our upbringing and character plus the constraints – economic, social, environmental, legal – that we face.

These two philosophers, our contemporaries, tell us that love is about this world and ourselves. They provide singular definitions of love and argue them with wit and fervor. Those definitions, different as they are, nevertheless make love natural, coming from within. No arrows strike love into the heart from outside; nor does God pour love into us.

But people *did* think otherwise, and many still do. In this book, I explore not what love *is* but how it has been imagined, to see which elements of those imaginings have been sloughed off and which remain to inspire us today and sometimes to get in our way. That is not to deny that the resolutely non-transcendental notions of love espoused by May and Frankfurt were true within certain emotional communities in the past and continue to be so (perhaps still more widely) today. Indeed, rejecting the enticements of transcendence was exactly what Homer had Odysseus do when he left the beautiful and seductive goddess Calypso and her promise of immortality in order to return home, to his aging and mortal wife. Few in Plato's day imagined that they had given birth to children – let alone that they might climb a ladder of loves – in order to transcend themselves and the world. But in some emotional communities Plato's idea did take hold, inspiring ways of living, feeling, and believing, both before Christianity and later on – within and without the monasteries that dotted medieval Europe. Not everyone cultivated a vision of love's transcendence in the medieval period, as we saw with Heloise, who put her hopes in a different fantasy of love. But many did. And it continued to inspire through the Reformation and into the nineteenth century, though then it derived from Plato's "first rung" – the family and children.

Back to the first rung

And today? Today, the love of another human being, erotic not parental, is for many the source of love's transcendent power. We can hear it in Wilson's high falsetto, aurally enacting his ascent. We hear it again at the end of *West Side Story*, where lovers Maria and the dying Tony sing in a mixture of grief and joy that there is, even after death, "a place" for them.[25]

But the idea is now unmoored from classical notions of virtue, or Christian visions of union with God, or (as we shall see in chapter 4) the troubadours' hopes of ennoblement through love. Rather, it is the expression of erotic ecstasy, which is inevitably short-lived. So it is that, after Bella and Marc Chagall float above the city, then "suddenly you had come down to earth again, looking back and forth from your painting to me. 'Still quite a lot to do, eh?'"[26] No transcendental love lasts forever, at least in this world. Even Plato knew that: he says that Socrates, on his way to the *Symposium*'s dinner party, "began to think about something, lost himself in thought, and kept lagging behind" (174d). This was a playful reference to the mocking image of Socrates in Aristophanes' play *The Clouds*, where the philosopher floats in a basket in the sky. But even Socrates eventually came down from his contemplation of beauty itself, if that was what he was doing, in order to tell the dinner party guests about the ascent. Bernard, too, exited the Bridal chamber and descended to talk to his monks. Porete glimpsed the total annihilation that awaited her, but she would see it in full only after her death, so she took time out to write about it for other "simple souls." Thomas Wright left off mourning his son and awaiting their reunion in heaven long enough to remarry and take a new job. Love has the potential to take us higher and higher, but, unless we recognize how fleeting such moments must be, we risk expecting too much of a good thing.

3

Obligation

"Love means not ever having to say you're sorry," Jenny tells Oliver in Erich Segal's immensely popular 1970s book *Love Story*.[1] The line was repeated in the movie that came out the following year. Was Segal, a classics professor, thinking of Odysseus' description of a marriage of like minds? Not likely, for the newly-weds Jenny and Oliver were not like-minded: he had just torn a phone out of Jenny's hands and flung it across the room. Those words about apologies were uttered when he subsequently repented. Later in the story, Oliver used the very same words to his conscience-stricken father, even though the two never once saw eye to eye.

No, the meaning is in the idea of "having to." Love obliterates duty. When you love someone, whatever you do is an act of love. "All you need is love," sang the Beatles, around the same time that Segal wrote *Love Story*.[2] But the idea was not the invention of the 1970s. Recall Heloise's reaction when Abelard proposed marriage in the twelfth century: she would rather be his "whore" than his "wife" because that would prove that her love had no ulterior purpose, committed him to no obligation. (Unspoken here, however, was her hope – as we saw in chapter 1 – that Abelard would nevertheless spontaneously love her unconditionally in return.) Think, even more radically, of the Christian God's love.

God was not at all obliged to love mankind. Indeed, he had every reason not to do so given the treachery of Adam and Eve in the Garden of Eden. And yet he cared about their sinful progeny so much that he sent his own son to be sacrificed to redeem them. God's love was and is gratuitous.

If all you need is love, then Jenny and Oliver's ultra-simple wedding vow – "to love and cherish till death do us part" – makes perfect sense.

Now imagine that the two had wed according to the rites that originated in England around the twelfth century and persisted long afterward, with vows similar to those that Heloise objected to. "Oliver," the officiant would have said in Latin, "do you want to have this woman as a wife, and love and honor her, hold her and guard her in health and sickness, as a husband should a wife; and leave all other women on account of her, and cleave to her alone as long as you both shall live?" And nearly the identical question would go to Jenny. Both would reply: "I want it." Then each would be required to make separate promises in the vernacular, very similar to those in Latin, although Jenny alone would have to swear to two extra obligations: "to be complaisant and obedient, in bed and at table."[3]

Here Jenny and Oliver are obliged to love and, indeed, to love each other exclusively. The wife, moreover, explicitly promises to satisfy her husband's physical and procreative needs.

Many commentators think that the 1960s and 1970s changed all that, bringing to full fruition what had been long aborning – love minus obligation. Viewing this from the vantage point of the twenty-first century, many of them think it a lamentable turn of events. Zygmunt Bauman speaks of it as "liquid love" that adheres to no one.[4] Jean-Claude Kaufmann thinks it spells the end of joyful love.[5] Stephanie Coontz argues that it has pulverized relationships.[6]

The fantasy is that there has been a big change from the past to the present, from taking explicit vows to insisting that all you need is love. I argue that, while it is true that love (I speak here of long-term love) came with obligations in the past, it still does so today. To be sure, there have been enormous changes in Western history, both in the nature of the obligations and in the meaning and feeling of love. Today, I argue, the obligations of "unobligated" love are, if anything, greater and more demanding than those enshrined in marriage contracts and the like. Love without obligation is supposed to mean that, when we love, whatever we do comes out of that love. Sometimes the result is the ironic obligation to do *everything* out of love and to expect our beloved to do the same. When and if what we do feels like drudgery, or when our partner says that what we expect from him or her feels like drudgery, we feel disappointed in love.

The misconception about love's obligations is the corollary of a misunderstanding of the history of Western marriages that traces progress from pure duty to full liberation. The modern fantasy is that people today, unlike past partners, marry (or form intimate partnerships) not because of external pressures – whether parental or cultural – but purely because they love. Therefore, marriages today are – or should be – unlike those of the past, which *were* most certainly constrained by outside forces and burdened with onerous duties such as "complaisance and obedience," whether in bed or out of it.

But past marriages were rarely so fully forced or obligated as we imagine (especially not for men); nor are our present loves so freely chosen or undutiful as we would like to believe. The obligations have changed; the ways in which love is felt and experienced have changed. That is the brief of this chapter. But the idea that "all you need is love," that everything that you and your partner do for each other today should be a gift of love requiring no "must" or "have to," is a mirage.

Greek patriarchies and their fissures

For seven years, Homer sings, Odysseus lived as the captive of the beautiful nymph Calypso with no "obligation" except to remain on her paradise island and make love with her. By day, like a dutiful ancient Greek housewife, Calypso sits at her loom and weaves; and, as her golden shuttle flies, she sings, like the sirens who lure sailors to their deaths with their wondrous, irresistible songs. At night, she and Odysseus bed down together, she eager for his caresses and "forever beguiling him with soft and wheedling words to forget his island, Ithaca" (1.56).[7] And yet, admittedly only after seven years of this seeming bliss, he sits "on the stony beach, rending his heart with tears and sighs and sorrows" (5.156–7). He wants to go home.

This is the model Greek man, married to the model Greek woman, Penelope, who remains faithful to him while he is away – first at war for some ten years, then for another ten on his homeward voyage, when he is detained by various adventures, including his liaison with Calypso and a year-long dalliance with Circe, another goddess. Twenty years absent, yet he is faithful to Penelope in his own way. Husbands might have love affairs – in *Works and Days*, Hesiod, writing around the same time as Homer, says that Odysseus and Calypso had two children, while Odysseus and Circe had three[8] – but they did not forget their wives. The obligations of matrimony were clear: virtuous husbands like Odysseus did not flaunt their affairs. And so, after he and Penelope at last reunite and make rapturous love, he recounts all his exploits to her – except for the amorous bits. Similarly, Odysseus' father refrained from having an affair with a female slave, "for fear of his wife's anger" (1.433). In their own fashion, these husbands respect their wives' feelings.

One reason why Calypso cannot convince Odysseus to stay with her is that he distrusts her – even after (perhaps especially after) she plays her trump card and promises him immortality if he will remain with her. That distrust is almost "built into" Western culture, explaining why some commentators, though not Homer, claimed that even Penelope had been seduced by one of her suitors. Although Homer leaves that out, he has the clever Odysseus reveal himself to his wife only after he is at last convinced that she has been utterly faithful to him.

All ancient Greek marriages involved a double standard. Homer made that clear early on, and it was true even for the gods. Calypso, a goddess and therefore not ordinarily subject to human laws, was forced by Zeus to let Odysseus leave her even though he and the other male gods could dally with all the women they liked.

The loyal Penelope resists sleeping with any man other than Odysseus. She could wed again, of course, and without reproach. Indeed, before going off to war, Odysseus told her that, "if the day comes when you see our son grown and bearded, then wed the man of your choice, and leave this house" (18.269–70). That day has almost arrived. Penelope's situation is desperate: competing suitors have taken up residence in her and Odysseus' home, feasting at their expense. They are destroying the household that gave meaning to Homeric "like-mindedness."

If matters were as they ought to have been, Penelope would be presiding over the indoor tasks – weaving, managing the household servants and slaves, and above all having and caring for their children. The wife's *raison d'être* was to produce children, and Penelope still might bear some; if she had married at the age of fourteen, as

did many Greek girls, she would still be young enough.
And the outdoor tasks – the livestock, vineyards, fields
of grain – would be under the supervision of her husband. Now neither spouse is doing anything right:
Odysseus is wandering and Penelope is weeping.

The rules of the game seem to be made for men.
Either Odysseus will come to put things right, or one
of the men of Ithaca will come and take her and all her
property to his own house. Or she will return to her
father – no doubt he arranged for her to wed Odysseus
in the first place – and he might choose another husband
for her. It seems, then, that women have only obligations and no freedoms in Homeric society. But a woman
like Penelope knows how to fulfill her role and still
find freedom's wiggle-room. She weaves, like a dutiful
housewife, but at night she unravels the cloth. It takes
the suitors nearly four years to catch on to the trick. She
keeps her options open by "toying with the passions in
the [suitors'] hearts, offering hope to all, making promises to each one, and sending them messages, but herself
planning otherwise" (2.90–2). She comes down to the
great hall where the men are, looking gorgeous, and
"at once the men's knees were weakened, their hearts
inflamed by passion: each one of them prayed he might
share her bed" (18.212–13). She even has her own way
to test Odysseus when he declares who he is to her: she
pretends that she has moved their bed. Only his fury at
hearing that about the bed that he had literally rooted to
the earth – by building it around a living olive tree – at
last proves his identity to her. Only then does she cover
him with tears, kisses, and embraces. She sees the gaps
in the prevailing patriarchy and uses them.

*

Marriages retained nearly the same obligations, rules,
and freedoms when Greece reorganized from the mon-
archies of Homer's day to the city-states of classical

Greece, and even when, by consequence, marriages ceased to serve the union of whole families in order to focus on the couple itself and its duties to the state. The main purpose of marriage remained procreation. Plato's *Laws*, which discusses the legislation needed to establish a new polity from scratch, declares that the first step in forming a city is "the union of two people in the partnership of marriage."[9] This is the building block of the city, the cell from which all else is generated. The couple's job, declares Plato, is to replenish the city's population. This was already a hackneyed idea: some half century before Plato, the Athenian leader Pericles had admonished his fellow citizens after they had lost many men in an early battle of the Peloponnesian War: "those of you who are of the right age must bear up and take comfort in the thought of having more children. In your own homes these new children will prevent you from brooding over those who are no more, and they will be a help to the city, too."[10]

Where is the love here? We glimpse it, amid many obligations, about a century later, in the dialogue on the household by Xenophon (d. 356 BCE), Plato's contemporary and a fellow disciple of Socrates. To discuss the joys and many duties of a gentleman's wife, Xenophon posits a model husband, Ischomachus, in conversation with Socrates. When she first arrives at his home, Ischomachus explains, his wife (never named) is a sheltered and untutored fourteen-year-old. But, after giving her a moment to adjust to her new life, he takes her firmly in hand, teaching her the tasks she has to master. Just as the gods command the "leader of the bees," the queen, to stay in her hive while she "weaves" the honeycombs, nourishes the young before they are fully grown, and sends out the workers to gather the pollen, so must a wife remain in her house. Her job is to prepare what comes through the door – grain for bread, wool for clothing, and the like. If she needs something from outside, she sends her slaves to fetch it. Within, she is in charge of keeping everything in order and in their proper place. She cares for the couple's infants, for the god "allotted to her a greater affection for the newborn infants than he gave to the man" (7.24).[11] By the same token, the husband's place is out of the house, supervising all the outdoor tasks. This division of labor, Ischomachus exults, works out perfectly: husband and wife are "partners" in caring for the household unit.

In this busy hive, love is a wifely obligation – if her husband is honest and straightforward with her, as she must be with him. Ischomachus explains, recalling the time when his wife applied make-up and wore high heels. She wanted to look pretty. Ischomachus would have none of it. "'Tell me, wife,' I said, 'would you judge me more worthy to be loved as a partner in wealth if I showed you our property itself [and] didn't boast of having more property than is really mine, . . . or if instead I tried to deceive you by saying I have more property than is really mine.'" His prudent wife promptly replies "'Don't you become like that; if you did, I for my part could never love you from my soul'" (10.3–4). She is obliged to love her husband – if he is honest with her.

But her husband, too, has the duty to love his wife if she does right by him, though Ischomachus says so obliquely. Since the two are "partners in one another's bodies," would he not (he asks rhetorically) be "more worthy to be loved" if he kept his body strong rather than smear it with vermilion color to appear more attractive? Yes, of course, and the corollary is that he will find *her* "more worthy to be loved" if she presents herself to him unadorned. His wife catches the drift – "I wouldn't touch vermilion with as much pleasure as I would you, . . . or see flesh color with as much pleasure as your own" (10.6–7).

The obligation to love is conditional, requiring exemplary behavior on both sides. This gives wives a chance to wrangle a better deal. And so the wife of Ischomachus coyly asks him if a wife is really the "leader" of her hive. "I wonder whether the works of the leader are not rather yours than mine. For my guarding that distribution of the indoor things would look somewhat ridiculous, I suppose, if it weren't your concern to bring in something from outside" (8.39). She is not going to get much pleasure out of the life he is painting for her, and they both know it. This leads him to assure her that some aspects of housework will please her. And then he offers a serious concession: she will get "the most pleasant thing of all" if she is so efficient that she seems better than he, for "you will have no need to fear that with advancing age you will be honored any less in the household" (8.43). The debilities and wrinkles of old age pose a grave issue for a woman who is a "partner" in her husband's body. The life-long honor that Ischomachus will owe his diligent wife offers her a bit of room to maneuver within the parameters of male domination.

*

Glimpses into the classical Greek household suggest that wives could indeed find the fissures in patriarchal arrangements, though they ran the risk of stretching the gaps too far. From an Athenian court case come the words of Euphiletus, a man charged with the murder of his wife's lover. His testimony recounts that,

> when I decided to marry and had brought a wife home, at first my attitude towards her was this: I did not wish to annoy her, but neither was she to have too much of her own way. I watched her as well as I could. . . . But later, after my child had been born, I came to trust her, and I handed all my possessions over to her, believing that this was the greatest possible proof of affection.[12]

Because his wife would have had to go downstairs every time she wanted to give their child a bath,

Euphiletus moved to the women's quarters upstairs. Their nuptial bed remained up there with him, but his wife often went downstairs to nurse and sleep with the baby. Eventually she took up with a lover there. We have no need to follow the rest of the story. The point is that, after a while a sort of trust developed between husband and wife that was strong enough to bend the rules of Greek domestic architecture, literally turning the house upside down. But apparently Euphiletus' wife overplayed her hand. Their sort of love, like that of Ischomachus and his wife, was utterly conditional.

The right match

The ascendency of Rome over the Greek world in the second century BCE shifted the emphases within long-term intimate relations. While Roman marriages had many similarities to those of Greece in Xenophon's day – the transfer of the woman from her father's house to that of her husband; the emphasis on procreation within a monogamous marriage in order to continue the male line; the double standard for sexual liaisons outside the marriage – nevertheless, Romans *explicitly* stressed the affectionate bonds that should attach husband and wife to each other.

The consent of both partners was necessary before a marriage could take place, and that consent had to continue for the duration of their life together or either party might initiate a divorce. From the mid-first century BCE on, perhaps because of an increasing emphasis on the individual and his or her happiness, Romans expected spouses to love (or at least feel affection for) each other. Loving families were the ideal: husbands and wives exchanged kisses, expressed tender love for their children, and missed each other when apart.

It was in this new atmosphere that the Stoic Musonius
Rufus (first century CE) and the moralist and biographer
Plutarch (d. *c*.120 CE) challenged the long-held view
that the main purpose of marriage was the begetting of
children. To be sure, "the birth of a human being . . .
is something marvelous," Musonius admitted, but for
that you needn't be married. No, "in marriage there
must be above all perfect companionship and mutual
love of husband and wife, both in health and in sickness and under all conditions."[13] For his part, Plutarch
identified a variety of marriages; the best – because it
was the most natural – was based on love: "A marriage
between lovers has [a] natural unity; a marriage for
money or children is made of units connected together
[like the rooms of a house]; a marriage based simply
on the pleasure of sleeping together is made of separate
units, and should be called cohabitation rather than a
shared life."[14]

These were high-minded words about marriage, but
what did they mean in practice? We may glimpse the
answer in some of the letters of Cicero (d. 43 BCE), the
Roman politician whom we met in chapter 1 writing
about friendship. During a period in which he was exiled
by his enemies and feared for his life and property, he
wrote to his wife, Terentia, who remained in Rome:

> When I write to you or read your letters, I am so over-
> come with weeping that I cannot bear it. . . . I long to see
> you, light of my life, with all speed, and to die in your
> embrace. . . . What am I to do? Beg you to join me, when
> you are a sick woman, prostrated in body and mind? Or
> should I not beg you, and as a result be without you? . . .
> Be assured of this one fact: so long as I have you, I shall
> not regard myself as utterly lost. But what will become
> of my fond [daughter] Tullia? . . . Then again, what is to
> become of my [son] Cicero? I cannot write more on this
> now, for I am choked with grief.[15]

A flood of tears was perfectly manly as an expression of affection between husband and wife. To see Terentia once more, to die in her arms: these passionate sentiments were written by a man wed already more than thirty years. They were certainly expressions of love, and mingling with them were obligations – his responsibility for his wife's health, both physical and spiritual; his care for his children; his unspoken certainty that, if he asked Terentia to join him, she would do so.

And indeed, in the same letter, he soon added explicit requests that he expected his wife to carry out. He knew that she was his political ally, exerting all her considerable influence to have him recalled to Rome, so he told her, "if there is a prospect of my return, you must strengthen and assist the process. But if, as I myself fear, the door is closed on me, then join me in any way you can." As was common in Roman upper-class marriages, his wife held her own properties separately from her husband's, but in a case like Cicero's she could be expected to keep an eye on his affairs as well. So he gave Terentia some instructions about their slaves: only one of hers should be freed, while the fate of his own would depend on his political fortunes.

Above all, Cicero was sorry to have to ask his wife to take care of their daughter Tullia's remarriage rather than see it through himself. Although he thought of Tullia as a child, she was in fact, by the time of this letter, nearly thirty years old and had already been married twice, having lost one husband to death and the other to divorce. She herself was an eager participant in the search for a new husband. We might say that the Roman pre-marital hunt for the right match was even more careful than the *New Yorker* cartoon knight's quest in figure 1, full as he was of prudent pre-rescue inquiries.

Why couldn't Tullia remain single? It was unthinkable in the context of Roman mores. It would have entailed her loss of reputation, another chance to find marital affection and happiness, and the possibility of having children to delight both herself and her parents. When, a few years later, Cicero lost faith in Terentia and divorced her, she too remarried, even though she was in her early fifties. It was nearly equally unimaginable for men not to wed, so Cicero, too, remarried, this time to his young ward. (Both that choice and the man Tullia eventually fixed on seem to have been rather incautious "love" matches, and neither turned out well.)

Of course, Cicero, Terentia, and Tullia were not "typical" Romans, and they mingled in the very highest social circles. Nevertheless, their lives and loves reveal some of the practices and ideals of their day. Like other husbands, Cicero did not flaunt his patriarchal authority but, rather, presented himself as caring about his duties to his family and regretting his inability to carry out his part of the bargain. Above all, he presented himself as a loving family man.

However, the turbulent political era of Cicero ended in the establishment of an emperor, Augustus, who, in the guise of making Rome great again, instituted new and strict rules for marriages. Under Augustus, it was not only unthinkable but also illegal for adults not to be married. Extra-marital sex and male–male sexual relations were criminalized, and childless couples were penalized. And love? The evidence is conflicting. The ultraconservative Dionysius of Halicarnassus, writing in the era of Augustus, emphasized power, not affection, citing the ancient practice that "compelled married women, since they had no other recourse, to live according to the wishes of the husband, and it compelled the husbands to control their wives, since they were a necessary and inalienable possession."[16]

Yet it would seem that the ideal of the loving couple persisted, as we see on tombstones, where both husbands and wives commissioned inscriptions that called their spouses "dearest" and on occasion "very loving." One particularly affecting epitaph from the third century (no doubt composed by the husband) had the deceased wife saying, "I was beloved, a modest and happy wife joined to a chaste [i.e. faithful] husband, but the envious law of fate rendered our vows fruitless and left me, poor loving wretch, only the consolation of being allowed to yield up my life in my husband's arms."[17] On the tombstone from c.80 BCE in figure 6, two freed slaves address each other for the edification of chance passersby. The husband, on the left, speaks first: "She, who died before me, was my wife, of chaste body, whose heart towards me was as loving as mine to her." She replies on the right:

> In life I was called Aurelia Philematium, chaste, modest, with no knowledge of the common people, faithful to my husband. My husband was my fellow-freedman, the same whom, alas, I am now without; in truth he was more than a parent to me: when I was seven years old, he took me on his lap; now I am 40 and I find death. He flourished through my dutifulness.[18]

On the relief between the inscriptions, the two clasp hands.

The love of children, too, was commemorated on Roman tombs, as we see in this inscription from the mid-first century BCE:

> Eucharis Liciniae
> Educated and trained in all the arts; a girl who lived 14 years.
> You there, as you look upon the house of death with a wandering eye,
> slow your step and carefully read our inscription,
> which a father's love gave to his daughter,
> where the remains of her body are buried.[19]

In the light of Augustus' imperial legislation, which persisted (with some modifications) for centuries, Saint

Perpetua's repudiation of family life (see chapter 2) becomes all the more astonishing.

Christianity's imprint

On the other hand, Perpetua's "rebellion" conformed to Christian teaching, one extreme of an initially non-Roman emotional community. As this group consolidated, expanded, and ever more carefully defined itself and its values, its notions of love ultimately overturned those of pagan Rome. The Church elevated chastity – defined not (as previously) as faithfulness to one spouse but, rather, as total celibacy – to the highest rank, as the best way to love God. Marital love came considerably below that, and love outside of marriage, according to the Church, was not love at all. But the Church did not speak for everyone, and, as we saw with Heloise and Abelard, and as we shall see again in chapter 4, love apart from marriage was lauded to the skies by some – perhaps by many – even as the authorities upholding the official line were laying down their strictures.

Christians read the words of both Old and New Testaments as commands. Genesis 1:28: "Be fruitful and multiply." Genesis 2:24: "Therefore a man leaves his father and his mother and clings to his wife, and they become one flesh." Exodus 20:12: "Honor your father and your mother." But, on the other hand, Luke 14:25: "Whoever comes to me and does not hate father and mother, wife and children, brothers and sisters, yes, and even life itself, cannot be my disciple."

It was Paul who first reconciled these conflicting rules by ordering them in a hierarchy. His letter to the Corinthians (1 Cor. 7) sets out the basic scheme. There Paul wishes "that all were as I myself am" – that is, unmarried and celibate. But if that cannot be, then, adapting the Roman law of his day, "each man should have his own wife and each woman her own husband. The husband should give to his wife her conjugal rights, and likewise the wife to her husband." "Conjugal rights" meant sex on demand. Paul mentioned one exception to that: times devoted to prayer. Finally, Paul discouraged divorce: "To the married I give this command – not I but the Lord – that the wife should not separate from her husband ... and that the husband should not divorce his wife."

Lots of obligations, then. But nothing on love? Yes. In the letter to the Ephesians (5:22–6:4), love itself was an obligation, though only of the husband, who took the place of Christ within the nuclear family: "Wives, be subject to your husbands as you are to the Lord. . . . Husbands, love your wives, just as Christ loved the church and gave himself up for her." Here marriage mirrors the entire machinery of salvation. It stands to reason, then, that Church councils tried to assume the task of regulating marriages. The letter to the Ephesians, though now thought to be by a disciple of Paul (let us call him pseudo-Paul), was considered authoritative, and canon law elaborated endlessly on the strictures initially adumbrated by Paul, pseudo-Paul, and the Church Fathers. At first, celebrating their own chastity, churchmen saw marriage primarily as a way to prevent the sin of fornication. Even then, they hedged marital sex with restrictions designed to limit its frequency and pleasure. Periods of abstinence included Lent, Advent, Easter, Sundays, and times of menstruation and pregnancy. Sex was legitimate only for procreation, and the less pleasure in it, the better – so, no unusual positions, no unnecessary fondling or kissing, and keep your clothes on. Chaste marriages were praised. Think of the two model lovers described by the sixth-century Bishop Gregory of Tours: married for life but never consummating their union sexually, their love for each other was so strong that, although buried separately, their tombs miraculously moved next to each other.

At first, much of this was of supreme indifference to most laymen and -women. Marriage was a family affair, and the Church had nothing to do with it. But this began to change as the parish system was gradually put in place and Church teachings seeped more deeply into the lives of ordinary people.

Meanwhile, the Church, too, was changing, slowly rehabilitating marital love. Increasingly the Church insisted on the public assent of both bride and groom, somewhat undermining parental control, and some churchmen began to claim that marriage was a "sacrament of love." This was at the very time when celibacy was being definitively imposed on priests and concurrently the chaste life (as we saw with Saint Bernard) was coming to have an erotic charge. Bernard's sermons lauding holy chastity mirrored the praises of love sung (as we shall see in chapter 4) by many in the world. To this heady brew of erotic talk, song, literature, and (no doubt) behaviors, churchmen added the sacrosanct relationship of spouses, proclaiming marriage to be the *only* place where real love, true love, between a man and a woman could reside. All else was lust.

Hugh of Saint Victor (d. 1141), an eloquent spokesman for this view, thought that the newly created Adam and Eve had been married in a "compact of love," instituted by God for the purpose of peopling the earth. That compact did not change after the Fall. Rather, to marriage's good purpose – namely generation – was then added the less good: marriage as a concession to the weakness of the flesh. The "mingling of flesh," otherwise utterly sinful, became honorable in marriage (though chaste marriages were still better). The love of husband and wife in marriage was "a sacrament and the sign of that love by which God is joined to the rational soul . . . through the infusion of His grace."[20]

Alongside this enhanced view of marriage came a new appreciation of the Holy Family and the bonds of love and caring that united it. We see this, for example, in a twelfth-century ivory carving (see figure 7) in which Mary, Joseph, and the baby Jesus are knit together by their enfolding hands and arms. Countless images of the Virgin suckling or playing with the Christ Child further speak to the divinization and sentimentalization of family life. Aelred of Rievaulx, who spoke so feelingly about the delights of like-minded friendships (see chapter 1), revealed the emotional import of the family in his day when he explained how to participate imaginatively in the lives of Christ and Mary:

> First enter the room of blessed Mary and with her read the books which prophesy the virginal birth and the coming of Christ. Wait there for the arrival of the angel. . . . Next with all your devotion accompany the mother as she makes her way to Bethlehem. Take shelter in the inn with her, be present and help her as she gives birth, and when the infant is laid in the manger, break out into words of exultant joy.[21]

Later in the story, he tells his reader to join the Virgin as she searches for the young Jesus in Jerusalem (Luke 2:48), bursting into tears of relief when she finds him, and so on.

This sort of affective identification with the scenes of Christ's life on earth led, about a century later, to Saint Francis' re-enactment, for the first time, of the manger scene in Matthew and Luke. And that, in turn, was part of a wider movement to stage, in real time, all the important events of the Old and New Testaments not only in the space of the church itself but around towns on feast days, when the entire population could come out to watch, shout encouragement to the Holy Family, and jeer at Christ's persecutors. From Germany comes a popular drama that completes the family circle, with Joseph as a most loving husband and father:

> Joseph (carrying the cradle): "Mary, I have considered
>   it well and brought you a cradle in which we can
>   lay the little child . . ."
> Mary (sings): "Joseph, dear husband mine, help me
>   rock the little one."
> Joseph responds: "Happily, my dear little wife."[22]

*

Naturally, it is one thing to peek into Christ's loving family and quite another to know what a real medieval household was like. Doubtless there was great variety. Yet it stands to reason that images of the ideal would both mirror and serve as models for earthly relationships. The holiness and indissolubility of the marital bond, the idea of conjugal debt, the injunction to have children, with its implied obligations to raise them to honor their parents and be good Christians – these matters were preached in church every week, and, after 1215, the laity was obliged to attend at least once a year.

Indeed, Ephesians 6:1–4 said explicitly: "Children, obey your parents in the Lord. . . . And, fathers, do not provoke your children to anger, but bring them up in the discipline and instruction of the Lord." And mothers? We see one early example in the ninth-century noblewoman Dhuoda, living in the south of France while her young son William was up north at the court of the king. The boy was serving as a hostage for his father, Dhuoda's husband Bernard, one of the most powerful men of the Carolingian kingdom, who had suffered a falling out with the king. Dhuoda wrote to her son, "anxious and filled with longing to do something for you." That "something" was a manual, full of prayers, poems, and precepts "for the health of your soul and body." She also wanted to remind William "of what you should do on my behalf."[23] She feared for all their lives and never questioned her husband's rights or decisions; she told William to honor his father after God; she had all her priorities straight. But, just by writing her manual, she asserted herself and her prerogatives, as a mother, to tell William how to lead his life. Her book spoke not only of her love for her son but also – and above all – of the obligations he owed to her. None of this changed the essentially patriarchal control that her husband had over her and their family. But it shows – as do other examples – how wives might push the boundaries of their assigned roles even as they fulfilled them.

Manuals were normally written by men – clerics – rather than by women. One such practical life-coaching book was Robert Mannyng's popular *Handling Sin* (1303), which used biblical and Church teachings to offer – in charming vernacular verse couplets – some of the ideals and normative social expectations in the England of his day. Familial love and its obligations came up often. Parents must love their children and should not curse them for little faults, while children should dread not heeding parental discipline. When the time comes for children to wed, parents should not try to enrich themselves but, rather, make sure that their offspring marry out of "steadfast love."[24]

Parents indeed stood to gain from a wealthy match, and perhaps many children did not object. Still, there were exceptions, as in the case of Margery Paston in the fifteenth century. Her family was of the English gentry – and particularly ambitious and on the rise. Nevertheless, she secretly married her family's bailiff and insisted (once her parents found out) that she had consented to the union, and, "if those words did not make it legally binding, she would make it" so right then and there.[25] Hers was a love match.

But *The Good Wife's Guide*, a manual presumably written by a man towards the end of the fourteenth

century, is not about love. The author professes to be a
well-to-do elderly Parisian husband anxious to instruct
his fifteen-year-old bride, not so much for himself (he
says) but "so that you can better serve another husband."[26] Like Xenophon's dialogue on the household,
but at far greater length, his book specifies all the things
his wife must master to ensure a busy, comfortable,
and well-appointed domesticity. When he tells her how
to train a hawk to seek its prey and then return to her
fist, we see that undergirding his surface lessons – in
gardening, cooking, entertaining, catering to her husband's needs, and lecturing her on the dangers of sex for
pleasure – is the one cardinal obligation: obedience. He
offers her the model of the ultra-patient and submissive
Griselda, a character introduced to the literary world by
Giovanni Boccaccio (d. 1375) and wildly popular for
centuries thereafter. In this story, as the author of *The
Good Wife's Guide* recounts with relish, the powerful
nobleman Walter chooses for his wife the good and
beautiful daughter of a very poor man. Before marrying
her, he asks that she swear to be obedient to him in all
things, without resistance "in word or in deed, in sign
or in thought." She agrees; in an age of increasingly
powerful lordships, the household is, in this story, to
mirror the state. To test her obedience and patience,
Walter takes away their babies, supposedly to kill them.
Like Job – even more fully than Job – Griselda shows no
resentment as her husband heaps woes upon her. At last
Walter pretends he has papal dispensation to divorce her
and take a new bride; Griselda is to prepare the nuptial
festivities. To all this Griselda dutifully complies, for, as
she tells her husband, "Anything that pleases you must
also please me." In the "happy ending," this untrusting
husband trusts at last, reveals all to have been but a test,
and reunites the family. Here the fantasy of obligation
has given way to a perversion, that of total control over
the other.

Some women internalized Walter's ideal, or at least preached it. Thus, even Christine de Pizan (d. 1430?), widowed early in life, able to support herself and her family on her own earnings as an author, and something of a proto-feminist, nevertheless concluded her book on "ladies of fame and women worthy of praise" with the admonition:

> You ladies who are married, do not scorn being subject to your husbands, for sometimes it is not the best thing for a creature to be independent. . . . Those women with peaceful, good, and discrete husbands who are devoted to them, praise God for this boon. . . . And those women who have husbands who are cruel, mean, and savage should strive to endure them while trying to overcome their vices.[27]

This parroted the official view.

But it was not the whole of the official view. Canon law also called upon spouses to care for each other. This requirement, which the law called "marital affection," along with the stipulation that bride and groom must freely consent to be wed, gave some wives (and a few husbands as well) the chance they needed to dispute their marriages before Church courts. Cases adjudicated in the episcopal court in Catania (Sicily) in the later Middle Ages reveal that husbands, too, had obligations: they were penalized for desertion, for failing to maintain their wives and children, and sometimes for committing adultery. And when two young people, Betta and Giovanni, disputed their betrothal, arguing that only their parents had agreed to it and that, as Betta put it, she had "never wanted to be betrothed or married to him and I did not want him and I do not want him," the court found the betrothal invalid.[28]

1. 'Before I Fight this Dragon'
New Yorker Cartoon
Maddie Dai's prudent knight upsets
our fantasies about valorous medieval
knights who risk their lives for love of
their lady.

*"Before I fight this dragon and rescue you, can I ask a few questions?
Like, do you want kids? What's your passion? Where is 'home' to
you? Do you have a financial philosophy?"*

2. Sergius and Bacchus
The military saints Sergius and
Bacchus were the best of friends
and (as their biographer said)
"undivided from each other." In
this icon from the 7th century, the
halos of the two saints and Christ
form a golden chain uniting them
in love.

(overleaf) 3. Marc Chagall, *The Birthday* (1915)
The kiss of Marc Chagall and his fiancée Bella on
his birthday flips him literally head over heels. They
float off the floor, about to escape their tiny room.

4. Old Testament Genesis, Initial

The startlingly empty roundel just below God signifies the Nothing that was apart from God at the moment just before Creation. The annihilated soul of Marguerite's *Mirror* is conceived as that very nothingness into which Divine Love may pour itself.

5. Lady Love Hits Her Mark

The arrow shot by Lady Love hits its mark on the panel to the left; on the right, the lover shows her his wounded heart. During the High Middle Ages, jewelry boxes such as these were sent by grooms to their prospective brides. Although their marriage had no doubt been arranged and the couple had not yet seen each other, the object symbolized their expectations of falling in love at first sight.

RELIVS·LL
ERMIA
NIVS·DE·COLLE
VIMINALE
AEC·QVAE·ME·FAATO
PRAECESSIT·CORPORE
CASTO
ONIVNXS·VNA·MEO
RAEDITA·AMANS
ANIMO
DO·FIDA·VIRO·VEIXSI
STVDIO·PARILI·QVM
VLLA·IN·AVARITIE
CESSIT·AB·OFFICIO
VRELIA·LL

AVRELIA·L·L
PHILEMATIO
VIVA PHILEMATIVM·SVM·
AVRELIA NOMINITATA
CASTA·PVDENS·VOLGEI
NESCIA·FEIDA·VIRO
VIR CONLEIBERTVS·FVII
EIDEM·QVO·CAREO
EHEV
REE·FVIT·EE·VERO·PLVS
SVPERAQVE·PAREIVS
SEPTEM·ME·NAATA
ANNORVM·GREMIO
IPSE·RECEPIT·XXXX
ANNOS·NATA·NECIS·POT
ILLE MEO·OFFICIO
ADSIDVO FLOREBAT AD

6. Roman Tombstone
On this inscribed stone funerary relief from *c*.80 BCE of Aurelia Philematium, a husband and wife express their mutual love.

7. Holy Family

The affective impact of this family portrait is hardly impaired by Mary's missing head. As Saint Joseph puts his arm protectively around his wife's shoulder and shields mother and child with his body, she in turn tenderly embraces their swaddled baby.

8. *The Lover Heard*, *c.*1785, Louis Marin Bonnet
In this print by Louis Marin Bonnet, an ardent suitor strikes a humble pose, while the lady cocks an ear and accords him a side-long glance. The print was so popular that it was adapted for mass production by a textile manufacturer in Nantes.

(opposite) 9. Eros (5th century BCE)
Eros flies in to visit a woman preparing for her nuptials.
Lightly touching her on the shoulder, he prepares to
crown her with a wreath. She is in love.

10. A Nun Gathers Penises from a Tree
Unlike the male protagonist of the *Roman de la Rose*, who wants just one
rose, the nun here is happy to have lots of penises in her basket. A bit later in
the manuscript she and the monk she is embracing here have a roll in the hay.

11. Castle of Love
On this small ivory roundel, probably a box cover, a castle populated
by ladies is besieged by lover-knights. The ladies defend themselves with
flowers and flowering branches. (Paris c.1320–40)

12. Roman Erotic Scene
Made during the reign of
Augustus at Rome, this cameo
glass perfume bottle shows
a man about to penetrate a
boy. On the other side the
man (perhaps the same one)
kneels over a woman, his arm
encircling her waist.

13. America Greets Vespucci

In the sixteenth century, Jan van der Straet prepared this sketch for an engraving (which is why the lettering is backwards). It was part of a series meant to illustrate new inventions and discoveries. Just landed in America (his ship beached behind him), Vespucci is greeted by a voluptuous, naked woman in a hammock, the first Miss America.

14. Aretino as Phallic Satyr
On the obverse is Aretino's head in profile. On the reverse, as if his mirror image, is this head of a satyr made up entirely of male genitalia. The penis near the eyes is ejaculating, a metaphor for the role of the gaze in exciting imagination and judgment, which, in turn, stimulates thought and speech – the semen of the mind.

15. Lord Byron
As Byron became identified with great lovers like Don Juan, he developed a cult following that has not yet disappeared: consider the many Byron portrait iPhone covers for sale. Here he is presented as a young ancient Roman with curly hair.

All you need is love?

In the eighteenth century, words of love were everywhere in the letters exchanged between husbands and wives and aspiring lovers alike. The movement of Europeans eager to explore, exploit, and conquer both the New World and Africa made letters frequently the only way to keep in touch; general literacy encouraged the practice; and the establishment of regular mail delivery services made it possible for couples even to court by mail. There was nothing new about gaining the *consent* of the beloved – that had long been necessary to make a marriage valid. Furthermore, the idea that love should *precede* marriage had for some time been a cultural ideal in some circles (we have seen flickers of it already and will see more in chapter 4). What was new in the Enlightenment, then, was the *general* belief that, to marry, a man and a woman should first love each other. And, at least in Protestant countries, where monks and nuns were chased out of their convents and ministers were expected to be family men, nearly everyone had to marry. At the same time, Protestant theologians insisted even more decisively than Catholic churchmen that marriage was a union of love. The result was that finding a mate to love became an obligation of sorts.

In the 1700s, love letters exchanged over years of courtship – handwritten with lavish care, on the finest paper that the correspondents could afford, filled with postscripts to express love's irrepressibility – witness to the sentiments that often served as the prelude to marriages. Those from men tended to be assertive, those from women more modest and tentative. Both were performing cultural models of masculinity and femininity with which to express their emotions (see figure 8). When people want to tell of their love and other feelings, even today, they generally look to well-trodden paths for guidance. This doesn't make the feeling any the less sincere – indeed, we can't be entirely original in such matters or we won't be understood. In the eighteenth century, there were plenty of available patterns. Some were in the form of copy books offering proper models for declarations of love leading to marriage; others were invitations to have an affair (see the next chapter). In every case, letters were key to the lovers' enterprise. Novels such as Richardson's *Pamela* and Rousseau's *The New Heloise* (*La Nouvelle Heloise*) presented their protagonists entirely through letters rather than narrative.

Yet not all written models for courtship were in letter form. *The Art of Courtship; or The School of Love*, with tongue partially in cheek, offers an oral dialogue between lovers Thomas and Sarah that starts with Thomas uttering, "O my love, how happy am I thus to meet you," and she replying prudently, "I am too wise to credit all that men say." As he presses his love, she stops beating around the bush: "Well, to be plain with you, Tom, for I cannot hold out any longer, if you love me, as you said you do, let us be married as soon as you will, and then do as you please. As for our fortunes, they are pretty equal, so never mind that." (Love here was clearly not the wise Sarah's only consideration.) Tom replies in ecstatic, if mediocre poetry:

> If you consent to [be] my charming bride,
> All cares I'll banish, and while by [my] side
> You panting lie, night shall thy blushes hide.
> Night, the covert of infant love,
> Shall make you know how dearly I do love.[29]

Clearly Sarah's obligations started with the bed, but they would continue with traditional household tasks. As Eliza Moode, a wealthy and well-educated young woman in mid-eighteenth-century Philadelphia, wrote to her friend about a man they both knew:

Does he think that all the business of our lives is only to learn how to make a sausage or roast a joint of meat and take care of a house and practice in short good economy? All that is necessary, I avow it. But can't we be that and take charge of our spirits at the same time; must we neglect the most valuable part for fear of offending our masters?[30]

"Our masters"! In the context of colonial America, which was filled with slaves and their owners, Eliza was using a very strong term indeed. Yet she admitted that it was indeed "necessary" that women care for the household. Like the exemplary wife of Xenophon and the dutiful one of *The Good Wife's Guide*, she accepted all those expectations even as she chafed at the idea that her life would be thus limited.

A half century before the Philadelphian Eliza was musing on the tasks of wives, Frenchwoman Madeleine de Scudéry (d. 1701) was able to live well enough on earnings from her novels to avoid marriage altogether. Nor did she wish to take a lover, with all its risks of heartache and the likelihood of pregnancy and children that it would bring in its train. Rather, she introduced and fostered the idea of an ultra-refined love, the friendship between a man and a woman that she called "tenderness." It did not culminate in bed. Even so, like seduction, it depended on ardent male pursuit. In her best-seller *Clélie*, the heroine offers a "Map of Tenderness" to her would-be lovers – or, rather, "friends." As in the children's game *Candyland*, the players must begin at the bottom: they start with New Friendship and must traverse a narrow path upward strewn with challenges. The goal is Gratitude and Esteem. Along the way the would-be friend must visit the cities of Submission, Love Letters, Respect, and many others – and avoid the path to Gossip or Fickleness, or (worst of all) drown in the lakes of Enmity or Indifference. At the top of the map is the Dangerous Sea and beyond it Unknown Lands – presumably lands where sex takes place. Created in an era when European exploration and conquest of the New World was all the rage – when John Donne could liken undressing his mistress to exploring America – the Map of Tenderness was one woman's pert answer to male fantasies. Men might (as Donne did) want women to "License my roving hands, and let them go, / Before, behind, between, above, below."[31] But Scudéry created a world in which those hands were tied – to writing love letters. The obligations in Scudéry's world – to travel smartly up the map or arrive at a miserable dead end – fell on *men*, while women judged whether they were moving in the right direction. At her salon, held regularly on Saturdays, Scudéry dressed up like the ancient Greek poet of love Sappho, while her male admirers wore costumes of other historical or mythical characters. It was more than a game, for it lasted for years; Scudéry's close friendship with Paul Pellisson, a fellow author, ended only with his death shortly before her own. But perhaps it may be likened to role-playing games today, at least those that require absorption, dedication, and postponed gratification.

*

Both courtship for love and Scudéry's courtship for tenderness neglected to state clearly what life would be like once across the Dangerous Sea – when one was actually married. In the nineteenth century, romantic novels such as Charlotte Brontë's *Jane Eyre* ended with "Reader, I married him."[32] Or, along with Gustave Flaubert's *Madame Bovary*, they explored the tragic consequences of a marriage that did not live up to the blissful expectations promised by novels and pretty picture books – "filled with love affairs, lovers, mistresses, persecuted ladies fainting in lonely country houses, . . . dark forests, palpitating hearts, vows, sobs, tears and kisses . . . and gentlemen brave as lions, gentle as lambs, virtuous as no one really is."[33] Emma Bovary – who, before marrying, thought she was in love with her husband – discovered that he was not the "white-plumed rider on a black horse" of her dreams but, rather, a dull mediocrity whose "conversation was as flat as a sidewalk." When she discovered excitement with a lover, she felt that at last she had entered the realm in which the heroines of novels lived in a "fever of happiness," and yet soon she was wanting "a ring, a real wedding ring, as a symbol of their eternal union." Life with her lover was not eternal and soon ended. But say it had been eternal; say they had lived together forever afterward. What then? Would domesticity with her lover have brought her the fulfillment that she craved?

Around the time that Flaubert was writing, white middle-class Americans, especially in the north, were crafting courtship rituals designed to ensure the happiness that Emma found so elusive, pinning their hopes on knowing one another's "true self."[34] As in the eighteenth century, they used letter-writing as an important medium of expression, but now, a century later, they were demanding much more than professions of love. They wanted self-revelation. "One of the greatest pleasures of my life has been the free outpouring of your thought and feeling," wrote Albert Janin to Violet Blair as he courted her. The editor of a model letter collection apologized for offering "exemplary" love letters, since "befitting writing can only spring from the deepest recesses of the human heart." A young woman pleaded with her reticent fiancé, "James, write it all out to me. Maybe twill be a relief to you. Let *me* share your troubles. Let me know them. I can feel for you." Here the obligation to confess merged with the fantasy of like-mindedness. Similarly, when the novelist Nathaniel Hawthorne courted Sophia Peabody in the 1830s, he claimed that her letters "introduce me deeper and deeper into your being, yet there is no sense of surprise at what I see, and feel, and know, therein. I am familiar with your inner heart, as with my home."

Catholics had long been used to confessing their sins; nonconformist Americans were accustomed to searching their souls in the sight of God, sometimes offering testimonials of their spiritual progress before an entire congregation. The Romantic movement, which started at the very end of the eighteenth century (see chapter 4), contrasted social conventions, public manners, and prescribed etiquette with "true" thoughts, private passions, and unfeigned sincerity. To the writers of nineteenth-century love letters, it was an obligation to contemplate and express their inner selves; to cultivate, in order to confide, their particular individuality. Kissing and petting became part of courtship rituals because sex, too, was understood as an aspect of self-revelation of both body and soul.

Notwithstanding their baring all, lovers (particular male swains) were often additionally required to pass tests to prove their unwavering affection. In a sense these tests acted in the stead of parental decision-making; women's doubts about the choices they "freely" made were assuaged by setting up ordeals meant to be valiantly surmounted. Thus, even after Violet Blair poured out her heart to Albert, she also tested him to the utmost, at one point pretending he had a rival, at another "sort of" breaking off their courtship, and at still another offering him pretexts to do so himself. He passed these challenges most ably. Even so, Violet foresaw trouble ahead: "What an unlucky letter 'M' is, to begin medicine, martyrdom, murder and matrimony – ."

She knew very well that, once a couple wed, their courtship obligations tended to end as each took on their prescribed gender roles: men excelling in public life outside the home, women tending the fires within. Most spouses were willing to distinguish between the excitement of romance and the settled existence of married life. But that did not automatically translate into contentment. In general, while men basked in the glow of domestic happiness, delighting in "a pleasant little home of our own," women tended to long for the promise implied by the courtship rituals – a companionate marriage, in which two people, having revealed their souls to each other, became partners in a common enterprise that ensured personal satisfaction for both. This rarely happened.

Starting in the 1920s, advice books, magazine articles, and novels began to offer new ways to retain the pizzazz of courtship and love affairs long after the wedding. World War I had wrought a seismic reordering of values and traditions, among other things liberating the "flapper woman." Even before that, Havelock Ellis' sexology and Sigmund Freud's psychoanalysis had given new significance to erotic life. In the wake of these changes, Marie Stopes' very popular book on marital sex told husbands to ride the monthly "love tides" of their wives. She included graphs of the ebb and flow of female sexual desire to explain when to make love and when to hold off. Husbands were advised to make each episode of intercourse a moment of "fresh wooing" – quite a contrast to the notion of conjugal debt or wifely obedience.[35] But while husbands were obliged to mind the tides, wives, too, had obligations: they must let their husbands have activities apart from them, and they themselves should cultivate interests beyond the home. Stopes foresaw a future family that would create not only children (she advocated birth control) but also a "superphysical entity" representing "the perfect union in love of man and woman." This was not, however, the "companionate marriage" that the self-revelatory love letters had seemed to promise some nineteenth-century women.

And, indeed, other experts and novelists of the postwar period looked to women to make most of the adjustments necessary for a marriage to be harmonious – to run the household within a reasonable budget, to withstand the temptations offered by an increasingly consumer-oriented society, and to heed the sexual demands of their husbands. Popular novelist, magazine contributor, and screen-writer Elinor Glyn did give men a few marital tasks: to "pay attention to your manners and to your courtesy. Think of the little things that would please your wife. . . . Try to remember the anniversaries which have sentimental meanings for her – bring her little presents, and above all *say* lovely things to her."[36] At the same time, she advised wives to be "invariably sweet and loving to him, so that no matter what tempers and caprices he experiences in his encounters with the many others of your sex, he will never have a memory but of love and peace at home." The old double standard; the old imposition of separate spheres – the man outside, the woman within the home. And yet Glyn was willing to put the blame on both spouses equally for an unhappy marriage, telling them that they *must* say they are sorry, they must "make it up," they must stop sulking.

*

The fantasy that love is all you need in fact involves two stories. The first is that only today do we associate marriages (or life-long partnerships) with love; the second is that, because of that love, what used to be obligatory – based either on patriarchal traditions or vows or both – should now be done automatically out of love. Those stories are based on misunderstandings of the past and the present. It is true that there was always the expectation of a division of labor: the domestic sphere belonged to the wife; work, travel, military service, public life belonged to the husband. But, along with those obligations, love was, on the whole, an expected *part* of marriage and sometimes its very foundation: Odysseus

chose his wife over the love of a goddess; Cicero was
bereft in exile without Terentia; pseudo-Paul imposed
love on husbands as a duty; the Church declared that
marriage was a sacrament of love; early modern courting couples exchanged letters protesting love; Marie
Stopes told husbands how to keep their passion going.
Of course, there were miserable marriages in the past,
forced and loveless (such as the one Betta and Giovanni
might have entered had it not been for her local Church
court), or marriages not forced but loveless even so (as
witnessed to by today's many divorces).

Today in the West, most people marry for love. But –
at least in the industrialized world – the sphere outside
the home belongs to both husbands and wives. In the
United States in 1948, 28.6 percent of the workforce
was female; in 2016 that figure had nearly doubled, to
46.8 percent. In 1975, mothers of children under three
years old constituted 34.3 percent of the labor force;
by 2016, that had climbed to 63.1 percent.[37] Yet, with
some privileged exceptions, both men and women have
not given up the expectations of the past. The problem
is that now the domestic sphere has become what Arlie
Hochschild calls "a second shift" for women, who
typically do most home and child care – on average two
hours more per day than men.[38] (Interestingly, a study
published in 2007 suggests that the burden of household
labor is shared far more equitably in gay and lesbian
than in heterosexual households.)[39] The term "second
shift" was coined by an anonymous woman interviewed
by Hochschild, even though that woman "strongly
resisted the *idea* that homemaking was a 'shift'. Her
family was her life and she didn't want it reduced to a
job."[40] She resisted it, but it was true – or, at least, that
is how it felt. Her "family was her life," yet she also had
a job outside the home – as if Xenophon's wife set (for
herself!) the tasks of both the house and the estates: a
queen bee *and* her worker bees all in one.

Many women today find the second shift to be not just labor but also what Hochschild has dubbed "emotional labor" – the requirement to "feel" in certain ways.[41] Gemma Hartley uses the term repeatedly in her book about the frustrations, anger, and sheer exhaustion involved in keeping house *and* working an outside job. She thinks girls are trained from childhood on (by their families, schools, and role models) to manage their "partner's emotions – anticipating needs, preempting displeasure, and keeping the peace."[42] She argues that women must take on all the detailed responsibilities of bearing and rearing children – even if their husbands offer to "help out" – and they must strive to feel cheerful as they do so, however exhausted or resentful they may be. They are play-acting, allowing expectations – their own and those of others – to manage their hearts. "Why do we place more value now on artless, unmanaged feeling?" asks Hochschild. "The answer must be that it is becoming scarce."[43]

The idea that love is all you need reached its apotheosis in the 1960s and 1970s. While the United States was fighting a much protested war and students in Europe were demanding educational reform, the ideals of "free love" and "inner authenticity" were being popularized. In the United States, managers touted the same values for work, as if the reality of expanding hours for labor and diminishing pay were side issues because work was "meaningful." "Do what you love" was the mantra of Silicon Valley.[44] The same self-interested promotion might be said of the "managers" of the "All You Need Is Love" ideology. The song itself was written and performed by a few young men; the novel *Love Story* was penned by a man who narrated it in the voice of a fictive male, Oliver. If we look more closely at that novel, we see that, in fact, Jenny accepted without question all that marriage to Oliver demanded of her: to give up her scholarship to study music, to support her husband while he was in law school, to cook dinner within their meager budget after coming home from work, and of course to change her name. But the conceit of the novel was that everything she did was motivated by love.

The powerful obligation *not* to feel obligated clashes with another ideal: the companionate marriage, which in effect asks both partners to share work, childcare, and housework. When that does not happen in the ways each partner envisions, then they ask themselves: does he/she really love me? Marjorie Hansen Shaevitz, author of *The Superwoman Syndrome*, admits that even she – whose book argues that women can do it all – at one point imagined that, if her husband "really loved" her, he would "see how hard I was working . . . and would come to my rescue with cheerful resourcefulness."[45] He didn't: rather, he complained that men like him were already doing a lot, were sick of women's complaints, and might well be ready to chuck their wives to "find someone else to take care of them." In effect, he was saying that, if she *really* loved him, she would appreciate all he did and stop nagging him to do more.

The ideal of Oliver and Jenny collides even more fully with the model of "confluent love" proposed by Anthony Giddens, which "presumes equality in emotional give and take." There are a lot of obligations in this sort of love, which depends on "the degree to which each partner is prepared to reveal concerns and needs to the other and to be vulnerable to that other."[46] This is even more demanding than the duties that nineteenth-century courting lovers imposed on each other, for it asks of love not only the revelation of the self but, as its "first priority," the "development of self." Giddens, writing in the late 1980s, calls it "pure love" and thinks that it is coming to characterize – and *must* do so, given modernity's emphasis on autonomy and individuality – the amorous lives of young people in his day. It is not necessarily monogamous but, rather, depends on partners accepting "'until further notice,' that each gains sufficient benefit from the relation to make its continuance worthwhile."

Giddens recognizes that the partner given that "notice" may – almost certainly will – suffer. Even within a committed relationship (he admits) anxiety reigns: one is always asking "whether she really loves me, or if I love her more." Still Giddens seems quite sure that the ideal is possible: the trick is to balance autonomy with dependency. As more recent research has found, however, reciprocity and mutuality are not necessarily the ideal for many modern couples even in Western societies; whether it is or not depends on age, class, sexual orientation, political convictions, religious beliefs, wider social networks, and many other factors. And even when confluence is the ideal, the reality of the "lived experience" rarely measures up.[47]

A few years ago, in a much discussed article, Alain de Botton tried to assuage the disappointment of couples who do not have a confluent relationship (let alone a romantic one) by deflating the very possibility. We need to abandon the notion "that a perfect being exists who can meet all our needs and satisfy our every yearning. . . . We need to swap the Romantic view for a tragic (and at points comedic) awareness that every human will frustrate, anger, annoy, madden and disappoint us – and we will (without any malice) do the same to them." This is the opposite of confluent love. It is an attempt to stamp out a fantasy – and perhaps all fantasies – of love without offering an alternative other than that our partner is the "'not overly wrong' person."[48]

The Netflix movie *Malcolm & Marie* (2021) offers a rejoinder to the non-obligatory love of *Love Story* less pessimistic than de Botton's solution. The protagonists, long a couple, are both professionals, he a newly successful film-maker, she an unsuccessful actress. At a VIP preview of his new smash-hit film, he had thanked all

involved – except for her. She nurses the hurt for a bit
and then (as would be demanded by a confluent relationship) she expresses her feelings to him. He apologizes.
But that is not enough, and the two spend much of the
movie alternately fighting – their words ever more cutting and hurtful – and trying unsuccessfully to "forget
it" and make love. Both have nourished fantasies –
which emerge in the course of their argument – about
what each owes the other and has not given. She has
offered him her all (indeed his movie was based on her
life); he should be grateful. He has helped her (indeed,
she was an addict when he met her); she should be grateful. The moral of the movie, if I may simplify, is that
love means remembering to say "thank you." Malcolm
and Marie cannot be entirely "vulnerable to the needs
of one another," as Giddens would have them, but they
also need not settle for the "good enough" partner of de
Botton. Each owes the other a lot, and they need to say
so – to themselves, to each other, and to the world.
    It's a start.

                              *

Marriage for love today founders on many obstacles,
large and small, but one of them surely is love's "non-
obligatory" obligations. Love as an ideal is a given in
marriage and has more or less been so in the Western
tradition ever since Odysseus returned to Penelope. But
duties have also been a given, often enunciated in wedding vows themselves. Now we live in a post-war world
of co-earning couples. The new situation demands fresh
vows, as it were, but the notion that we should need
no vows at all ironically reinforces the old traditions,
in particular leaving the domestic space to women.
Indeed, during the pandemic of 2019–20, "one in three
employed mothers reported that they were the main
caregiver [of their children] compared with only one in
10 employed fathers. . . . And children spent more than

twice as much time with telecommuting moms than with their dads. Telecommuting fathers increased child care on telecommuting days, but not housework."[49] Even Xenophon knew that childcare and homecare were serious and important jobs, and the advent of telecommuting has rendered the distinction between homecare and work "outside" largely moot for many couples. New vows may not be the remedy for old habits, but they might be helpful. Today's obligations need relevant foundations, including transformed notions of manhood and womanhood and adjusted notions of the workplace. Taken together, "work" is ripe for reallocation and "obligation" is ready for redefinition.

4

Obsession

Penelope's endless tears express her love for Odysseus. They water the couple's nuptial bed as she awaits a return that probably will never happen. Only the bard's listeners know that Odysseus is on his way home. Prolonging Penelope's sadness, Homer makes her absolutely the *last* to know that her husband has arrived in Ithaca. Her steadfast fidelity to the memory of her husband is her most salient feature.

Her model persists. In the early 1940s, when Bess Gornick's husband died, she took to a couch from which she hardly moved for years (though she did, by necessity, to go to work). She wailed, she groaned, she hardly talked, she rejected all solace. "Mourning Papa," writes her daughter, Vivian, "became her profession, her identity, her persona."[1] Bess was in her mid-forties, capable and smart, yet with her husband's death she had lost all hope of future happiness. She was still bewailing her loss as she approached her eighties. At that point Vivian reproaches her: "you *wanted* to stay inside the idea of Papa's love. It's crazy! You've spent thirty years inside the idea of love."

Staying "inside the idea of love" is not a trait of women alone. Consider that "When a man loves a woman / Can't keep his mind on nothin' else." The man of this song is obsessed with this woman. And even though she is very much alive, he is already anticipating losing her and becoming wretched: "She can bring him such misery / If she is playing him for a fool." Sung by American Percy Sledge and the number one hit in 1966, the song's sentiments resonate today, as attested by the posted comments following a live-in-concert YouTube performance: "You can feel the pain in his voice. Absolutely transcendent," with 32 Likes; "This song touches my soul every time," with 493 Likes; "This is how I love my wife," with 323 Likes.[2]

Misery, ecstasy, and preoccupation. "I must be in love," says Jane Austen's Emma as she ruminates about Frank Churchill: "'I certainly must,' said she. 'This sensation of listlessness, weariness, stupidity, this disinclination to sit down and employ myself, this feeling of every thing's being dull and insipid about the house!'" The syndrome was as well known to ancient and medieval physicians as it was to Austen. It was called lovesickness. Today some scientists liken it to addiction.

Obsession disparaged

Despite the model of Penelope, the ancient world generally disapproved of and even ridiculed the sort of love that we associate with romance, the sort of love that we mean when we say that we have "fallen in love." Women were weak (thought the Greeks), so of course they were susceptible to it. But men were supposed to be stronger. In Plato's *Symposium*, one of the speakers is the gate-crasher Alcibiades. He arrives drunk, jealous, furious, and miserable because he is obsessed with Socrates. He is, he says, swept off his feet by Socrates every time he hears him speak – "my heart starts leaping in my chest, the tears come streaming down my face. . . . Nothing like this ever happened to me. . . . My very own soul started protesting that my life – *my* life! – was no better than the most miserable slave's." These are astonishing words coming from an Athenian aristocrat of great wealth and social standing, himself the master of many slaves. All he wants is to be around Socrates, yet it's anguish to be so. "Sometimes, believe me, I think I would be happier if he were dead. And yet I know that if he dies I'll be even more miserable" (215e–216c).[3] Long before, when he was confident of his own charms, Alcibiades had imagined that Socrates wanted to be his mentor and lover. Wonderful: he would aid and abet the wooing. Yet even after arranging for Socrates to pass a night at his place, even after crawling under the blanket to caress the older man, they "went no further than if I had spent [the night] with my own father or older brother!" (219d). How humiliating! Alcibiades' love is messy and unseemly. Socrates, the lover of transcendent beauty, remains calm – the clear winner of this game.

*

If Alcibiades felt ashamed by his overwhelming and unrequited love for another man, imagine how much more shameful it was for a man in ancient Greece to be passionately in love with a woman, especially if that love were illicit. It upended the right, the cosmic order of things. The choice of a bride was, as Xenophon knew, a family matter. Only when she was about to wed might the bride herself properly be overcome by love. That's why, in figure 9, Eros can place a wreath on the head of a young woman at her nuptial preparations. At any other time, a woman's passionate love had to be the result of magic spells or aphrodisiacs, interventions by outside forces. They required counter-attacks through alternative magic and witchery.

Some doctors, a minority, took a different view. They argued that love came from within. It was a disease of soul and body akin to (indeed, a form of) melancholy, the effect of excessive black bile, one of the bodily humors that fashioned human physiology. As Aristotle or one of his followers wrote, "those who possess a large quantity of hot black bile become frenzied or clever or erotic or easily moved to anger and desire. . . . Many, too, if this heat approaches the region of the intellect, are affected by diseases of frenzy and possession."[4] Later, in a Romanized world, Galen (d. *c*.200), whose writings would be fundamental to later medicine, claimed to have found good cures for those tormented by erotic desire:

> I know men and women who have been struck by passionate love and become despondent and sleepless, then contracted an ephemeral fever because of something other than their love. . . . When we discovered that what consumed them is love, we proceeded without telling them, let alone others, about what we had discovered, to prescribe for them bathing, drinking wine, riding and amusing visual and aural spectacles, and we . . . aroused [their] indignation about an injustice, love of rivalry and the desire to win over others, depending on each person's interest in the pursuit he has chosen for himself.[5]

In this pleasure-seeking and highly competitive society, amusements, honor, and glory were good cures for a lover's malady, the *real* source of which was so shameful and painful that even the afflicted refused to admit it to themselves.

Amusements, honor, and glory might do the trick; but many Romans by Galen's day valued, even above and beyond those, self-discipline and duty. Indeed, we might almost speak of two emotional communities of lovesickness at Rome, one valuing it – playful, painful, insouciant, obsessive, and stupid all at once – and the other rejecting such love as frivolous or even insane.

We see the first on display in the work of the Roman poet Catullus (d. *c*.55 BCE), written around the time that Cicero was penning his letters to Terentia. Catullus

honed his literary skills on the intimate details of a
love affair with his "Lesbia" – so called after the island
Lesbos where Sappho plied her own poetic skills.

> Let us live and love, my Lesbia . . .
> Give me a thousand kisses, a hundred
> . . . until we ourselves lose track of the score.[6] (5)

When their affair runs aground, he grouses that "No girl
will ever be loved more than she." All the worse for her.
He himself will be resolute:

> . . . Steel yourself.
> Girl, Catullus has now steeled himself.
> Farewell! Rejected, he makes no appeal. (8)

In an epigrammatic poem he sums up the lover's
condition:

> I hate and I love. You ask me why? Who knows?
> But I feel it occur and I'm tortured. (85)

Yet at exactly the same time as Catullus was revealing his emotions in all their messy turbulence, the poet
Lucretius (d. c.55 BCE) was ridiculing erotic passion. An
Epicurean, he accepted the fact that "a thousand kisses"
was a natural part of life, but no one should let it disrupt
their tranquility of mind. Thus "yearning to copulate
and ejaculate" is fine, but not when "that honeyed drop
of Venus' sweetness" is followed

> by chilling care. For even if your loved one is absent,
> images of her are with you and the darling name keeps
> ringing in your ears. It is advisable to shun such images,
> to abstain from all that feeds your love, and to turn your
> attention elsewhere: you should ejaculate the accumu-
> lated fluid into any woman's body rather than reserve it
> for a single lover who monopolizes you and thus involve
> yourself in inevitable anxiety and anguish.[7]

Except for the part about "any woman's body," an
invitation to indiscriminate sex, this was the voice of

the future. Pretty much the last gasp of the emotional community that valued "all that feeds love" came early in the next century, when Ovid (d. *c.*17) and a few like-minded poets rebelled against the legal strictures of Augustus, with his penalties for the unmarried and his criminalization of adultery. Thumbing his nose at such stuffiness (and suffering exile for it), Ovid wrote with a keen awareness of love's power to drive us crazy alongside an equally lively appreciation of the sheer fun of flirting, bedding, wasting away with desire, and eventually getting over it and moving on: "Okay, then, I confess. I admit to Cupid that I am his prey, his victim, and stretch forth my hands to be bound" (1.2, 26–7).[8] He's in love with "Corinna." She's married, and she is bringing her husband to a banquet the poet will be at as well. He is consumed with jealousy, but he has a plan: "Arrive before your husband," he tells her:

> He will pat the couch to invite you to sit,
> and you will do that, although in a modest, ladylike way,
>   but now and again you may touch my foot with yours,
> in secret, of course. And look in my direction sometimes,
>   to see my nods and the language of my eyes. (1.4, 21–5)

In a later set of poems, his *Art of Love*, Ovid tells men how to seduce women, giving instructions to help the predatory male; and to women he explains how to be seductive, though "I'm not saying, Go and get laid / By all comers, but, Don't be afraid."[9] That latter advice was still pretty much for the benefit of men. But Ovid was not unfeeling when it came to a woman's point of view. Imagining how Dido, the mythical queen of Carthage, felt when abandoned by her Trojan lover Aeneas in order to found Rome, Ovid endows her with utterly sane and yet passionate words in a poem-letter purporting to be from her:

I suppose you will manage to find a second Dido there
  [in Rome],
    another to whom you can give your meaningless
    pledges.
... And even if all this should happen just as you plan,
  how will you find a woman
    to be your wife and love you as much as I?
I am ablaze with love, a wax flambeau that is dipped in
  sulfur to burn all the brighter.[10] (28–35)

Ovid's Dido reveals her penetrating understanding of the psychology of a man who has not only left her for greener pastures – his duty, as he called it – but also abandoned his first wife, whom Aeneas "inadvertently" left behind when he fled Troy with his son and aged father.

By accident, was it? On purpose? I never thought to
  inquire,
or to pay any heed to what should have been fair
  warning. (129–30)

Yet Ovid was not entirely at odds with Lucretius, for he accompanied his books on love with another on the *Remedies* for love, telling men (and women too) to try not to fall in love in the first place. But, if they do, they should occupy themselves with business, or take long trips, or remember all the lies she told, or convince themselves that she is ugly, or sate their lust with another woman. Had Dido read his remedies, she

  might have been able to shrug off Aeneas
when she saw the Trojan sails disappear into the
  offing.[11]

In part because he here disparages passionate love and shares in the general misogyny that had always dominated ancient male attitudes, in part because of his poetic artistry, Ovid remained school-room reading throughout the Middle Ages. His poetry was a model for love letters between medieval students and teachers, most famously those exchanged by Abelard and Heloise (see chapter 1), and his amorous works were reflected in the medieval literature of romantic love. But there we get ahead of our story.

For if Ovid was the last gasp of obsessive love (and some stabs at curing it) in the ancient world, the steadfast and dutiful Aeneas was the wave of the next millennium. In the hands of Virgil (d. 19 BCE), Dido "on fire, . . . raved in frenzy through the city" (4.300).[12] But Aeneas, though he was admittedly in love with Dido, "burned to get away, to leave that land of pleasure" (4.282). Listening to the command of the gods, he calculates how he might most easily escape his commitments to her. On board ship, not quite ready yet to sail off, he falls asleep and dreams that Mercury tells him to get away – and fast:

> Can you sleep in such a crisis?
> Are you crazy? Don't you see the dangers all
> around you, or hear the helpful west wind blowing?
> [Dido's] plotting treachery and terror, she's set
> on death and feeds the surges of her rage.
> Won't you get out while you can? (4.560–65)

Aeneas awakens and calls his men to unfurl the sails. He is off to found Rome, where, in time, will reign

> the man you hear so often promised to you,
> Augustus Caesar, born of gods, who'll bring
> a golden age to Latium. (6.792–93)

Obsession exalted

Christianity scorned the hopes of Virgil; its "golden age" was in another world. It insisted on shifting the goal of love from earth to paradise (see chapter 2). For many it succeeded. But starting in the eleventh century (or, at least, bubbling up then into the written literature of the time) came a new conception of this-worldly love, the sort that its practitioners called "fine love" (*fin'amor* in the vernacular of southern France). It was passionate and frankly erotic, yet at the same time restrained and playful. It was so worthwhile that the man (and, sometimes, the woman) who felt it was granted a kind of nobility. The fine lover outdid in virtue and greatness of soul anyone who claimed elite status based on blood and inheritance. His fine love committed him to serving his beloved, even to the end of his life, even if she were cold and rejecting, even if his love gave him great pain.

Or so went the songs and stories of fine love. Their clever rhymes, meters, melodies, brilliant word play, and endless variations arouse admiration today but also, perhaps, provoke a gnawing question: did this literature express "real" feelings? The short answer is Yes. The better answer is that fantasies such as fine love are like molds into which feelings are poured. They may be "misused" – exploited insincerely or in jest or with the intention to abuse or simply to entertain. But they may also be employed because they work, they fit, they express something real. At the same time, fantasies are *unlike* molds in that they themselves create what they shape: feelings need words and stories with which to express themselves. They make use of bits and pieces of the values, institutions, and vocabularies of their ambient societies. In the age of the troubadours, ideals and words of fidelity, service, worship, subordination, and dominion were ready to hand for fine lovers to give voice to obsessive passion.

And so, from southern France, where the troubadours first sang, fine love spread to other European countries, where it took on different hues – the gentle heart (*cor gentil*) in Italy, the adventurous knight in France, the singer of *Minne* (Lady Love) in Germany. It thumbed its nose at the Church's restricted idea of love even as it found ways to incorporate religious imagery and feeling into its expression. It even percolated in turn into the pious sermons of clerics such as Saint Bernard, as we saw in chapter 2.

The practitioners of this new sort of love came from all ranks. Some were aristocrats themselves, keen to enhance their nobility "by blood" with nobility "by love." Others were entertainers from lesser social levels, patronized by great lords and ladies. All found audiences to delight in their jokes, allusions, and clever versifications, bask in their sentiments, and enter momentarily into their heartaches and joys.

A paradigmatic example of the troubadour's fine love is "It is no wonder if I sing" (Non es meravelha s'eu chan) by Bernart de Ventadorn (fl.1147–70 or 1170–1200), a poet who probably came from a family of the lesser nobility:[13]

> It is no wonder if I sing
> Better than other troubadours,
> For I'm more drawn to loving
> And better made for its command.

Bernart (or, at least the persona he has created) "sings better than other troubadours." We still have the music for this song, copied out in one of the earliest instances of written music and often re-created today.[14] Love is what gives the poet the genius to write a poem that still dazzles with its meter, rhyme, and strophic movement. He boasts that the reason he bests all other troubadours is because he's better at following love's "commands." What he means is that

> My heart (cor) and body (cors), knowledge and mind,
> And strength and power I give;
> The rein pulls me so hard toward love
> That I never look to other things.

Because the force of love is so strong, he has given himself over to it, heart and mind, body and soul. He celebrates his dedication. He is a bit like Alcibiades in being love's slave, but he is entirely different from Alcibiades in thinking that his very virtue lies in this servitude. So Bernart continues:

> He must be dead who cannot feel
> The sweet taste of love in his heart,
> What is it worth to live without valor,
> And bring only boredom to people?

In Bernart's day, valor ordinarily was the attribute of a warrior, a knight, a nobleman. Here a poet claims it for himself.

Moreover, he is a good and loyal knight, not treacherous like so many others in Bernart's world: "In all good faith, without deceit / I love her, the fairest and best." But in that there is a problem: how will his lady know that he is a true lover and not just a seducer? He wishes that there might be some clear sign; he would like for betrayers and false lovers to wear "horns on their foreheads!" He would give up all the wealth in the world (not that he has it) "Just so my lady would know for certain / How truly it is that I love her." But she really should figure it out anyway as soon as she takes one look at him:

> The glow in my face, my color, my eyes,
> For just as a leaf shakes in the wind
> I tremble all over in fear.

Yes, this love of his makes him tremble. And worse: it drives him to tears, for his lady is not responding as he would wish: "What more can I do, imprisoned by Love / In a cell, while she keeps the key?" Unlike Galen's lovesick patients, so embarrassed by their feelings, Bernart is wild to admit and embrace the experience of love with all its highs and lows:

This love strikes me so gently
In the heart with its sweet savor,
A hundred times a day I die in pain
And revive with joy a hundred more.

Cupid's arrow strikes: what bliss! To be lovesick is to be the best one can be: "My bad is better than another man's good."

And what does he ask in return for this love? It seems that love is reward enough in itself:

Good lady, I ask you nothing at all
Except to make me your servant,
For I'll serve you as I would a good lord,
And never ask for another reward.
So here I am, at your command,
A frank, humble heart, courtly (cortes) and glad!

Ladies, lords, and servants: they were utterly familiar in Bernart's southern France and elsewhere in much of Europe. Servants were supposed to "love" their lords and ladies; lords and ladies were supposed to "love" their servants in return. At the court of one great patron of troubadours, the count of Toulouse, terms of love were regularly used to refer to subordinates: the count's official documents, anything but dry, spoke of his "love" for his "faithful men" who supported him in wars; he loved the men in his service at court; he loved the citizens of his favorite towns and the monks at his favorite monasteries. In the classic ritual of vassalage, one way in which this sort of love was pledged, the vassal kneels, places his hands joined in prayerlike clasp between the hands of his lord, promises to be his faithful man, and then rises so that the two may kiss each other on the mouth. Kneeling was the posture that would later be adopted for the proposal of marriage (see figure 8). And, like that wooer, Bernart hopes to share the lady's bed:

I think now I shall die
of the desire I have
if the beautiful one there where she lies
does not bring me close to her,
so that I may caress and kiss her
and take to me
her white body, round and smooth.

It is just possible that the poet was saying he wanted
to marry this lady – certainly when he claimed to have
given his heart and mind, body and soul to love, he
was playing on the words of the normal marriage vow
used in southern France: "I give myself to you." But, in
Bernart's poem, "play" is the operative word: at its end,
he hopes "she'll forgive me for staying away so long."
He hasn't even been around the woman he so ardently
desires. What he really celebrates is not her but his own
wonderful and tormented experience, his utter surrender to unfulfilled desire.

That was true in many troubadour songs, where
erotic hopes were rarely realized. Jaufre Rudel (fl. 1125–
48) sang of his "far off love" (amor de lonh). Other
troubadours recounted how cruelly their ladies spurned
them, driving them into a winter of despair.

Such were the men's perceptions of their unwavering love. But the female troubadours (the trobairitz), of
which there were more than a few, had their own take
on the men they loved in turn. They too gained virtue in
loving, and so they loved openly and joyfully – though
often, like the men, they were forced to lament love's
treachery. Even then their love itself was so worthwhile
that it made love's pain a matter of pride. Here is the
singer La Comtessa de Dia, who, like Bernart, was probably a member of the lesser nobility in the latter half of
the twelfth century:

I'll sing of him since I am his love,
But I feel so bitter I'd rather not.

I love him more than all the world,
But mercy and grace do me no good,
Nor does my beauty, merit, or wit.
I've been deceived and betrayed
For no reason, and in spite of my charm.[15]

Like Bernart, La Comtessa is a song-writer and a singer
(we have music for this song),[16] and her feelings, though
bitter, urge her to sing. She loves – still does. But nothing avails – not her mercy (*merces*; has she slept with
him?), nor her grace (*cortezia*; she is the model of good
behavior), nor her fine looks, worthiness, or good sense.
Her lover has been deceitful. Even so, she continues,
"I comfort myself that I've done no wrong to you."
She is the better, the truer lover. Rather than saying
"Farewell" (as Catullus did, though he probably didn't
mean it either), she takes comfort in the very power of
her love.

Troubadours and *trobairitz*, ever the entertainers,
sometimes playacted a battle of the sexes. Here's Maria
de Ventadorn and Gui d'Ussel in a sing-song debate, a
bit like Annie Oakley with her future husband Frank
in *Annie Get Your Gun*.[17] In "Gui d'Ussel, I am concerned" (Gui d'ussel, be.m pesa de vos), Maria starts
things off: should a "lady in love do what her lover asks
her, just as he would do in return"?[18]

> GUI: The lady should treat her lover
>   As he does her, with no thought of station,
>   For lovers are equal, and neither is greater.
> MARIA: Gui, a lover should request
>   Gently what he desires;
>   And a lady can command
>   . . .
> And the lover must do whatever she asks.

Against Gui's egalitarianism, Maria declares that a
lover who swears to serve is *beneath* his lady and at her

command. They dispute a bit more, but Gui gets the final verse, upholding the subversive notion that lovers should be equals. Tongue-in-cheek yet serious, this song overturns the patriarchal order.

Obsession critiqued

The fantasies spun by Bernart and La Comtessa are utterly different from the one that Virgil gave to his hero Aeneas, who hardly thought about Dido once his ship set sail. It is even more radically unlike Origen's idea of love (see chapter 2), where bodily desire is disdained as sullying and dangerous to one's soul. Nor does it claim the like-mindedness that Heloise had with Abelard or Montaigne with La Boétie. Yet all those fantasies of love persist today, with all their accretions and contortions, wrenched out of context, and still continuing to work their magic – for good or ill.

But the fantasy that love is *obsessive* is unlike all the others above all in calling itself into question, sometimes even mocking itself. Imagine Virgil problematizing Aeneas' behavior, or Origen wondering if there were not something strange about fleeing earthly attachments, or the Church playfully querying the obligations of marital couples! Those ideas of love were serious and sure of themselves.

The poetry of the troubadours and *trobairitz*, like the *New Yorker* cartoon in figure 1, was willing to muddy its own waters by serving up – amid professions of undying love – feelings of anger and often playful mockery of its own premises. So Bernart's "fairest and the best" might possibly be – though he hopes not – "a lion or bear who'd slay me when I surrender." Maybe she's not so fair after all!

*

As the poetry of fine love spread to other parts of Europe, it was refined, reworked, and critiqued in new ways. It was also remade in new genres – above all romances (long poems of knightly adventures) and sonnets (each of fourteen pithy lines). Sometimes its later avatars were playfully critical of its very assumptions. Consider one of the manuscripts of the very popular *Romance of the Rose*. Its illustrator – very likely Jeanne de Montbaston, the wife of the scribe – used some of the lower margins to satirize both the idealized sentiments of the text and personages of supposed piety in society at large (see figure 10). On the left, a nun gathers penises from a tree. On the right, she embraces a monk. The pun of this pictorial commentary is all the more effective because the poem is about a man trying to pluck one particular rose, the focus of his erotic desires. The nun has an easier time of it: she doesn't care which penis she gets, and the more the merrier. Fabliaux – brief, often raunchy ditties aimed at both courtly and urban audiences – were equally burlesque, as they mocked clerics struggling with enormous erections and husbands easily cuckolded by wives. Such representations of the bawdy and obscene will proliferate in the next chapter, which takes up insatiable love and its equally avid search for new erotic experiences.

In a way, obsessive love, too, is insatiable, albeit focused on one particular beloved. That focus continued to be the case in the many serious explorations of love that proliferated throughout Europe in the twelfth and thirteenth centuries. The counterparts of the itinerant troubadours in Germany, the *Minnesänger*, echoed the original themes of love's joys and sorrows and unswerving service, yet sometimes they boldly challenged its very premises. If fine love is ennobling, sang some *Minnesänger*, then the lady must herself be noble by virtue. Virtue by definition should bring joy. If loving a lady brings pain in its wake, then why persist? In one song, *Many a person hails me* (*Maniger grüezet mich*

alsô), Hartmann von Aue (*fl.* 1180–1220) turns his
back on the court and its ladies, declaring that he is sick
and tired of "standing before ladies protesting my loyal
devotion." He's determined to look to "poor women"
for love. Among them, he will find one "who wants
me around." And "she shall be the delight of my heart,
too."[19]

A bit later, Hartmann's compatriot Walther von der
Vogelweide (*fl.* 1190–1230) tells his lady that "love is
the joy of two hearts. If they share equally, then that is
love." These *Minnesänger* doubt the "fineness" of fine
love. How can it be fine when it brings nothing but pain?
Sometimes, Walther meekly retreats: "Oh no! why am
I talking like this, blind and deaf as I am? How can a
man see when he is blinded by love?"[20] Nevertheless, in
other songs he flirts with a relatively new ideal – not fine
love (*hôhe minne*) but "equal love" (*ebene minne*), the
dream of mutual feeling.

*

By contrast, rather than call into question the ennobling
power of fine love, poets in Sicily and (a bit later) Tuscany
elevated the lady so far above them that they could only
gaze at her in awe, praise, and wonder. In Sicily the poets
were not itinerant; they worked as civil servants, nota-
ries, or courtiers at the court of Emperor Frederick II, one
of the most sophisticated and worldly-wise rulers of the
medieval period. Although Frederick was also the very
ruler for whom many of the *Minnesänger* in Germany
worked, his Sicilian "school" often had a very different
slant on love. In the poetry of Giacomo da Lentini (*fl.*
mid-thirteenth century), for example, expressions of pain
and disappointment take second place to his sense that
words are inadequate to express his feelings:

My passion
cannot be expressed in words,

for the way I feel it,
no heart could conceive nor any tongue could tell.[21]

Words are weak for Giacomo in part because he divinizes his lady: the joy she gives him outdoes the bliss of Heaven.

Without my lady, I would not want to go [to Paradise],
the one who has blond hair and a shining brow,
for without her, I could not have any joy,
being separated from my lady.

Giacomo, unlike Bernart, is not thinking here of the joys of his lady's body "round and smooth." To the contrary, he wants to be in heaven together with her

in order to see her dignified bearing
and the beautiful face and the sweet gaze,
for I would consider it a great consolation,
beholding my lady standing in glory.[22]

For this Sicilian poet, the lady is a heavenly vision.

It is not far from Giacomo to Dante (see chapter 2). And, indeed, Giacomo was probably the inventor of the sonnet, which was developed still further by Dante and, above all, by Petrarch (d. 1374). But Dante was also influenced by his *central* Italian predecessors, especially the Bolognese Guido Guinizelli (*fl.* second half of the thirteenth century), who asserted the superiority of the noble heart (*cor gentil*) over any other sort of high station or nobility. For Guinizelli, in contrast to the troubadours, it is not fine love that ennobles a man; it's the other way around: "love seeks its dwelling always in the gentle heart." It is the very nature of a noble heart to love, just as it is the very essence of fire to be hot. In his "Love seeks its dwelling always in the noble heart" (Al cor gentil rempaira sempre amore), the lady is simply the match that lights the fire. Just as God inspires the heavens to know and obey its creator, so the beautiful lady ignites the "desire which never ceases to obey her" in the noble heart. Will God object to Guinizelli's likening the movement of the stars to the lover's desire? Not at all! Guinizelli will be able to answer God right back: "She looked like an angel from your kingdom."[23] The lady here is hardly human.

The Florentine Petrarch (d. 1374), the most famous and influential of the vernacular love poets, claimed (like Dante) to have fallen in love with his lady, Laura, in his youth. Like Dante, he ascribed great significance to their first meeting and to her death exactly twenty-one years later, and much of his poetry was written to celebrate her. In his *Scattered Rhymes* (*Rime sparse*), his themes are the familiar ones of obsessive love: its pain, its yearning, the service it demands, the perfections of the lady it celebrates, the virtue it bestows on him for loving her. New in Petrarch is the layering of poem upon poem in one book – 366 of them – leading the reader to follow what Petrarch presents as the whole course of his inner, intimate, emotional life. This – along with his particularly sensitive use of the sonorous qualities of Italian – inspired contemporary composers to create musical adaptations. During his lifetime only one or two poems were set to music, but the sixteenth century saw an explosion of compositions, most notably in the *New Music* (*Musica nova*) (*c.*1540?) of Adrian Willaert, which used twenty-five of Petrarch's sonnets in a song cycle that, in its mournful tones, mirrored Petrarch's poetic melancholy: "When it is bright day and when it is dark night, I weep at all times. From fate, from my lady, and from Love I have much to grieve me."[24]

Yet Petrarch may never have known a Laura. She was above all a woman of fantasy and contemplation, utterly beautiful, wholly disdainful, the cause of the poet's eternal heartache. His voice cannot rise so high as to reach her ears. He burns with desire when he cannot see her, and writing about her makes his love all the more intense. Even so he cannot stop; his poetry is like Guinizelli's gentle heart, needing his lady to spark it into being. With the Italian poets we see how fine love, still an obsession, has nevertheless been transposed from bodies to phantoms.

*

Writers of medieval romances, however, did not trade in angels or phantoms. They told stories, often based on originally oral Celtic tales about the knights of King Arthur's court. These are the model knights that appear in fairy tales; one of them eventually turns up in Maddie Dai's *New Yorker* cartoon (figure 1).

Aristocratic patrons paid romance authors to explore in lengthy poems the ramifications of fine love and its claims. Did fine love justify adultery? Was it compatible with marriage? It is often said that in the poetry of fine love the beloved is so far above the lover that marriage is unthinkable. That's not so: it is certainly *thinkable*, as when La Comtessa de Dia declares to the man she loves, "Know that I'd like to hold you as my husband,"[25] and when Bernart used language from the marriage vow in his song of "the fairest and best." In many romances weddings are the normal and *logical* outcome of love. But when the knight and his beloved are married, a new issue arises: how can the knight reconcile the obsessive love he has for his wife with the obligations he has as a ruler and warrior? If a man in love "can't keep his mind on nothin' else" (Sledge), then how can he run a kingdom? Or spend his time away from home, fighting evil knights and giants? Or be devoted to his friends? Or act faithfully on behalf of his vassals below him or the lord whom he serves? Or worship God with fervor? All of those things are worthwhile and legitimate; all should work together seamlessly. But a husband in love has a hard time attending to them. And his wife has dilemmas of her own. How can she reconcile passionate love

for her husband while at the same time protecting her
honor and his? How can she keep him with her while
allowing him to take off on the adventures that are his
raison d'être? Passionate love tends to overrun its banks.
Romances offer modes of mastery and control for their
readers or listeners to try on and, often no doubt,
discard. They are among the medieval fantasies that
continue to charm today, not least in Disney movies.

In Chrétien de Troyes' *Erec and Enide* (*c.*1170),
the hero, one of the knights of the Round Table, is
handsome, valiant, generous, noble, and praised by
all. When he meets and falls in love with Enide, she is
beautiful and virtuous, though impoverished – rather
like Griselda (see chapter 3). But when Walter married
Griselda he immediately started to test her love. Erec is
different: he is overcome by love for his wife:

> But Erec loved so ardently,
> he burned no longer for events
> of knightly valor, tournaments;
> he showed indifference to them all
> and lived, absorbed and sensual,
> making [Enide] pet and paramour,
> still serving and attending her,
> kissing, embracing, dallying,
> seeking her ease in everything. (2432–40)[26]

His men begin to mutter. He never leaves his wife's side,
never carries out bold deeds.

> The knights deplored his injured name,
> the loss, the grief, the waste, the shame. (2457–8)

Enide hears their murmurs and tells Erec about them.
Then, as if love is either all or nothing, Erec rejects her
violently. Forcing her to ride ahead of him as he goes off
to seek "adventure," he makes her play the spy who will
see every danger before he does. Yet he forbids her to
speak unless he speaks first. When she dares to warn him

of oncoming marauders, he spurns her. He has become like Walter in testing her love. At the same time, he is trying to undo his shame. Meanwhile, Enide remains utterly loyal to her husband, and when she thinks he is dead, she tries to kill herself. After Erec revives, he realizes that she truly loves him, and he promises

> Henceforth have no anxiety:
> I love you as I never have,
>
> . . .
>
> Henceforth it will be my desire
> to live as we lived formerly –
> at your commandment I will be. (4904–10)

But this turns out not to be true. Rather, he has learned to integrate both her and knightly valor into his life. He loves her, but he also defeats evil enemies, inherits his father's royal throne, and does what kings must do, starting with offering charity to the poor and the clergy and continuing with a renewal of his fellowship at King Arthur's court.

Or consider Iwein, another knight at King Arthur's court. In Hartmann von Aue's version of the story, the hero is smitten by the beautiful Laudine: "love confused his senses, and he forgot himself completely" (1301).[27] Hartmann gently mocks the man in love, nursing wounds "supposedly more painful than those inflicted by a sword or a lance" (1519). After Iwein weds Laudine, his good friend and fellow courtier Gawein takes him aside to warn him of the fate of Erec, "who because of Lady Enite [i.e. Enide], idled about for a long while. If he had not recovered later and done what a knight should, his honor would have been forfeit" (2763). Iwein listens and takes off with his friend, but first he offers his solemn promise to Laudine that he will return within a year. At that point, he and she are so in love that "they exchanged hearts between them" (2971). But his friendship with

Gawein is so delightful, and the sporting life that they
lead so attractive, that Iwein entirely forgets his wife.
Hartmann blames Gawein: one can love a friend too
much, just as one can love a lady to distraction. When
Laudine confronts Iwein after the year is up, he sounds
the depths of human depravity: he goes wild, tearing off
his clothes and running "naked across the fields toward
the wilderness" (3221). Only after accomplishing many
deeds of valor does he find a way to return to Laudine.
Now their love is measured and calm. As Hartmann
comments, both are young and free of dishonor: they
have "become companions who can and will hold to
each other – and if God lets them live long lives – they
will have many a sweet moment" (8137). Theirs has
become a temperate love.

The adulterous love of Tristan and Isolde, the most
popular of medieval romances then (and now), had
many incarnations. In an Old French version of the
story by a late twelfth-century poet known as Béroul,
the love potion that Tristan (here Tristran) and Isolde
mistakenly drink, and that drives them to their obsessive
love, wears off after three years. Then the couple seeks
the help of a hermit to help reconcile Isolde with her
husband, King Mark. As Isolde explains:

> Never in my life will I again
> have any sinful desires.
> Please understand that I am not saying
> that I regret my relationship with Tristran
> or that I do not love him properly
> and honorably, as a friend.
> But he is entirely free of any carnal desire for me,
> and I for him."[28]

The poet knows that this is not entirely true, but he
doesn't care. He is a champion of these two faithful
lovers, Isolde so beautiful and good, Tristran the best
warrior who ever lived. Yes, love overruns its limits.

How unfortunate! But also: how fantastic! It calls forth the highest fidelity of which human beings are capable – as well as their cleverest lies and most heroic deeds on behalf of each other.

The admirable nature of Tristan and Isolde's love is even clearer in other versions, far better known today, though not in the Middle Ages. In these, the potion lasts for life, and the love of the two is so true, intense, and all-consuming that there is no resolution for it except death in an eternal embrace. Poet Gottfried von Strassburg (*fl.* 1200–10) explains why he has labored long and mightily to tell the tale:

> If the two of whom this love-story tells had not endured sorrow for the sake of joy, love's pain for its ecstasy within one heart, their name and history would never have brought such rapture to so many noble spirits! . . . For wherever still today one hears the recital of their devotion, their perfect loyalty, their hearts' joy, their hearts' sorrow – This is bread to all noble hearts. . . . Their life, their death are our bread.[29]

In John 6:35, Jesus said, "I am the bread of life." But, for Gottfried, love of the sort that united Tristan and Isolde is the bread of life for the man of noble heart.

A rapturous and utterly adulterous love is also featured in *Lancelot*, written for the wealthy patron Marie de Champagne by Chrétien de Troyes. The hero and Guinevere, the wife of King Arthur, share a love so intense and so pure that it virtually excuses them from censure. Thus, when at last they consummate their love:

> Her love-play seemed so gentle and good to him,
> Both her kisses and caresses,
> That in truth the two of them felt
> A joy and wonder,
> The equal of which had never
> Yet been heard or known.[30]

Here adultery is hardly an issue. Far more pressing in this romance is the hero's willingness to risk his very life – even to sacrifice it – for his beloved. He is akin to Christ when, in his pursuit of the kidnapped Guinevere, he crosses a bridge as sharp and narrow as a sword: crawling across it, he wounds his hands and feet, mirroring the wounds of Christ and the stigmata miraculously received by Saint Francis around the time *Lancelot* was written. In Chrétien's telling, Lancelot's obsessive love makes him an object of veneration yet, ironically, also an absurdity; his fine love leads to feats of obedience and service that every real knight would consider dishonorable.

And thus, even as poets and romancers celebrated the marvels of fine love in their various ways, they opened the door to criticism. Many authors accepted the invitation – sometimes ponderously in treatises and Church pronouncements, sometime lightly, in parodies. Oddly enough, the same patron might support both the literature of fine love and attacks against it. Consider the Latin treatise written by the chaplain Andreas.[31] He worked for Marie de Champagne, the countess who commissioned the love stories of Chrétien; but, unlike Chrétien, Andreas was no romance writer. The purpose of his work is bitterly contested, but it can hardly be claimed to promote fine love. Dividing the topic into two parts, a "pro" and a "con," Andreas turns the idea of love into a contest. In the first part he presents not seductive words but, rather, hard arguments that men should use with women of every class to tempt them to enter into non-marital love affairs. For each argument he offers a generally negative or non-committal reply that the woman should use. In a second section, Andreas retracts the whole idea of adulterous love, declaring it immoral, ill-advised, and foolishly lavished on the foulest of all possible beings – women. If your sexual itch is too strong, OK, find a wife, but don't imagine that love is involved in that! The only good love is for God. Despite its masquerading as a treatise on love, Andreas' work was an old-fashioned screed against all but religious love, a throwback to the era before churchmen such as Hugh of Saint Victor celebrated the holy love of matrimony (see chapter 3).

Obsession ritualized

Already in Andreas' work obsessive love had become a "style," a way to pay court to a lady, and she to answer him, without anyone really feeling much of anything. It was a game. And, indeed, the idea of love as a playful battle between men and women was widespread in Andreas' day, illustrated and sometimes acted out in pageants portraying a Castle of Love (figure 11).

Another game was played at the "Courts of Love" presided over by ladies. Andreas claimed that Countess Marie was foremost among the judges. If such courts were really held, they certainly had no jurisdiction. Nevertheless, according to Andreas, they handed down peremptory decisions, stripping fine love of its spontaneity and hedging it about with rules, ritualizing every move. Here fine love mimicked and even surpassed the contemporary meticulousness of Church law surrounding marriage. A brief sample of the courts' decisions gives the flavor of the corpus: "A woman sins against the nature of love itself if she keeps back her embraces from her lover . . . unless she has clear evidence that he has been unfaithful to her." If two absolutely equal suitors offer their love at about the same time, "in such a case the man who asks first should be given the preference; but if their proposals seem to be simultaneous, it is not unfair to leave it to the woman to choose." "Any woman who wants to have the praise of the world must indulge in love [with a lover]."

As if the court decisions were not enough, Andreas listed thirty-one rules decreed by the "King of Love," among which were these:

1. Marriage is no real excuse for not loving [someone else]. . . . 16. When a lover suddenly catches sight of his beloved his heart palpitates. . . . 26. Love can deny nothing to love. 27. A lover can never have enough of the solaces of his beloved. . . . 30. A true lover is constantly and without intermission possessed by the thought of his beloved. 31. Nothing forbids one woman being loved by two men or one man by two women.

Hemmed in by rules, railed against in diatribes, sentimentalized in "Saint Valentine's day, when every fowl comes there to choose his mate," the overwhelming passion of fine love at its origin was tamed.[32] It had always been under control, of course – fine love was by definition love purified through discipline, service, and the virtue wrought by the lady. But by the fourteenth century – even while never quite losing its cachet as a mode of real emotional expression – it had become above all simply the sign of the good manners of a courtier.

Thus, in his *Decameron*, Giovanni Boccaccio (d. 1375) created a well-mannered gathering during the plague in Florence. Ten young people, all noble, intelligent, courteous, and witty, escape the city for ten days in the countryside. "Under the rule of Pampinea" or one of the others, they take turns telling tales – some bawdy, some tender, many critical of the clergy, all diverting. They sing love songs and dance together, then retire to their separate rooms. Even though some of them are in love, they remain "afar," modeled on Petrarch's hopeless love of Laura.

Boccaccio's fantasy court lasted for a few days. Baldassare Castiglione (d. 1529) purported to describe a real one, the court of the duke and duchess of Urbino, in his *The Book of the Courtier*.[33] It boasted men skilled "in jousts and tournaments, in riding, in the handling of every sort of weapon, as well as in revelries, in games, in musical performances." They were there for the duke's amusement; real wars in the fifteenth and sixteenth centuries were fought by mercenaries with guns and cannons. The court's atmosphere was competitive, but its keen edges were made gentle, according to Castiglione, by the duchess. "We all felt a supreme happiness arise within us whenever we came into the presence of the Duchess. And it seemed that this was a chain that bound us all together in love." The men at court, he claimed, were like brothers. With the ladies, with whom they were allowed to mingle freely, erotic longing was absent. The "games and laughter" of the court's mixed company in the presence of the duchess had lots of "witty jests," but above all they were played out "with a gracious and sober dignity."

The seventeenth through early nineteenth centuries saw the rise of salons in Italy, France, Britain, and Germany. Presided over by *salonnières* – wealthy, accomplished women whose mastery of animated conversation raised "sociability" to a fine art – they attracted prominent writers, philosophers, artists, musicians, and diplomats. The lively exchange of ideas in mixed company or (in Britain) in female gatherings was de rigueur, and so too were semi-concealed love affairs. As the Dalmatian writer Miho Sorkočević admiringly characterized the learned Venetian hostess and writer Isabella Teotochi Albrizzi (d. 1836), she was "pure sensuality tempered by noble decorum."[34] Indeed, Teotochi Albrizzi, who of course was married, cultivated a number of lovers at the same time. Salons such as hers were the places to prod and test the boundaries of social, emotional, and political norms. They, alongside clubs, theaters and cafés, were the incubators of revolutionary thought and of the passionate emotional expression that historians have dubbed "sentimentalism." Yet Teotochi

Albrizzi's love affairs hardly celebrated *obsessive* love. Was that fantasy over?

Obsession regained

Not at all. For at the same time as Teotochi Albrizzi was entertaining, mentoring, and patronizing a coterie of international talent – and taking a few lovers on the side – the culture of Romanticism was aborning. Although to some extent reviving the romantic themes of the Middle Ages, the sort of love celebrated in the age of Romanticism did not poke lighthearted fun at itself. Its obsessions overran the confines of meter and rhyme. Instead, they flowed into a relatively new literary form – the prose novel. These explored the social lives and feelings of people living right then – in the time of their authors and readers. As Charlotte tells her suitor Werther in Goethe's *The Sorrows of Young Werther* (1774), "I like those authors best in whom I rediscover my own world, whose experiences resemble mine, and whose stories are as interesting and touching to me as my own domestic life."[35]

When Charlotte mentions one novel by name, Oliver Goldsmith's *Vicar of Wakefield* (1766), Werther has such transports of feeling that "I forgot myself completely." Werther, a young poet, sees nothing but benevolence in Charlotte (Lotte). He first meets her in an idyllic domestic setting. Her mother recently deceased, she has taken on that role for her younger siblings. Since that meeting (Werther reports in one of the letters to his friend that make up most of the book), "I don't know whether it's day or night." With Lotte, "I feel my own life and all the happiness ever given to a human being." He is tormented with inexpressible feelings – "a fainting in all my senses" – whenever the two touch by chance: "it's as if in every nerve my soul was turned about." In the mornings and nights, he reaches for her in bed, dreaming that he is covering her hand "in a thousand kisses." When the outfit he had worn at his first meeting with Lotte wears out, he gets another exactly the same – knee breeches, yellow waistcoat, blue overcoat. He finds happiness when he climbs the pear trees in the orchard and hands the fruits down to Lotte. She forms his prayers and populates his imagination; "everything in the world all around me I see only in relation to her." No troubadour could be more enthralled or offer his services more readily.

But there is nothing of the troubadours' playfulness in Werther. He tries staying away from Lotte for a while, then follows his heart and returns to her. Meanwhile she has married Albert, the man her mother had her promise she would wed. Werther imagines what bliss it would be to take Albert's place. He reports that "sometimes it is beyond my comprehension that any other man can love her, is allowed to love her, since I love her solely, with such passion and so completely and know nothing, understand nothing, have nothing but her."

There is something of the Raskolnikov in Werther. His "passions were never far from madness," he rather proudly admits, since he believes that madness is the mark of an extraordinary person. Before Lotte weds, he carries Homer with him; afterward, he turns to Ossian, a poetic pastiche of oral and written Celtic epics that was all the rage in Goethe's day. He is especially taken with a girl in the poem who "grieves herself to death" at the grave of her fallen lover. Werther sinks into bleak depression and finally borrows Albert's pistol and kills himself.

The effect of this book was electric. It was translated, adapted, and ridiculed. Men dressed in replicas of Werther's outfit, and women wore "Eau de Werther." Frankenstein's monster admired Werther as "a more divine being than I had ever beheld or imagined," applying the hero's unhappy condition to himself.[36] So many people committed suicide in imitation of Werther that sociologist David Phillips coined the term "Werther Effect" to describe copycat suicides. Although Goethe later claimed that he hadn't meant Werther to be a hero, his book begins with a prefatory note to the reader by its fictional "editor": he has gathered all of Werther's letters "and know that you will thank me. His mind and his character will compel your admiration and your love, and his fate will compel your tears." Goethe knew that his fiction could have real-world effects.

The originality of this romantic fiction was not that being in love is painful; Homer knew that well enough. Nor that love can become an obsession; Ovid had remedies for that. Nor even that people may die of unrequited love; that's why doctors such as Galen were called in to cure lovesickness. No, the novelty of Goethe's romantic fiction, although building on traditions long in place, was that a man in love will go to any length – *should* go to any length – if he is truly in love. Werther writes in his suicide note to Lotte: "It is not despair, it is the certainty that I have suffered my fill and that I am sacrificing myself for you." And a woman? Should she feel similarly? At the end, when the "editor" recounts Werther's last encounter with Lotte, the answer is clear. Yes! They will meet and love each other forever in "[God's] everlasting sight in eternal embraces." So, if Goethe has it right, a woman, too, will go to any length, at least in feeling, even though, to her lasting unhappiness, she is unable to slip the constraints of social arrangements like marriage. In nineteenth-century operas, women were as driven mad by love as were the men – with correspondingly tragic results.

Werther and other romantic novels, plays, operas, and poems offered the lessons that Flaubert's Emma Bovary (see chapter 3) learned to her peril. The particular story that Emma found most affecting was *Paul and Virginia*

(1788) by Jacques-Henri Bernardin de Saint-Pierre. Set on an island far from the corrupt civilization of Europe (riffing on Rousseau), the novel offers two protagonists who grow up together, fall in love, and desire to wed. But their pure and innocent love is undone by the materialistic values of civilized society. Virginia is called to France by a cruel but wealthy aunt, who disrupts the natural dénouement of love. When she is at last free of her aunt's terrible demands and on her way home, Virginia's ship is caught in a storm. "Naturally" modest, she refuses to shed her clothes and drowns. Paul soon wastes away and dies. Emma's thoughts dwelled on their happier days, when Paul climbed a nearby tree to fetch Virginia some delicious fruit – much as Werther gathered pears for Lotte – and forever offered her sweet love in their tropical wonderland. These were men attentive to a woman's every want. No wonder Emma poisoned herself when that was the romantic model. Flaubert knew, long before I ever had the idea, that fantasies can shape hopes, thoughts, and expectations, sometimes helpfully but sometimes also to our peril.

The fantasy in real life

This was certainly true for some unhappy Italian women living in the south of Italy in the 1870s. Consider Raffaella, the estranged wife of Captain Giovanni Fadda. When the circus came to town, she fell in love with its star acrobat, Pietro Cardinali. We know about these two and others as well because Pietro murdered Fadda and his trial became a cause célèbre.[37]

Everyone by then expected to marry for love, but what did that mean for young women whose families were vigilant to protect their virginity and limit their opportunities to meet men? Raffaella recalled her courtship thus: Fadda was "presented at home, we mutually liked each other," and he asked her to marry him. Thus did she join a legion of discontented housewives in nineteenth-century Italy.

Whatever the particulars of her and Fadda's domestic unhappiness, Raffaella was not alone in seeking romance elsewhere. Pietro Cardinali was the star of a circus that boasted exciting shows and body-revealing performers. He was the toast of many of the most well-to-do families in the towns that the circus visited. A handful of women fell in love with him and thought that he loved them in return. Or, at least, so they wrote in letters in which (mainly pseudonymously) they seemed to pour out their feelings. These letters must have meant something to Cardinali (possibly sentimental, possibly as grounds for blackmail) because he kept them in a locked trunk. They offered a way for women to "try on" and explore feelings that were normally taboo.

In one letter, evidently responding to his ending their affair, one woman wrote, "Beloved Pietro, I know that many women have loved you, but it is impossible that any of them could have loved you more than I do." In another from a different woman, "My dearest love, finally after thirteen days I've received your letter ... You know how much I love you and naturally you must know that withholding your news [i.e. not sending a letter] has the same effect on me as death." One woman sent him thirty-eight letters. Hoping for an eternity of love, she imagined that "God will render us happy with a sacred knot so as never again to be divided unto death. I will always be faithful. Tell me, my love, that you love me. That you will always be the same." And then a momentary doubt: "Should I have faith in your promise? For pity's sake tell me the truth." Soon he is asking her for money, which she hesitates to give him. When he stops writing to her, her reproach comes straight from the playbook of obsessive love as elaborated from the troubadours to her day: "What wrong have I ever done you that you treat me like this? It isn't done when you truly love. The thing you have always promised me was to love me forever."

*

Today few women in the Western world are so cosseted by their parents that they cannot meet many men, have a few affairs, break up, suffer, and move on. Unhappy marriages can end; people can find new mates or partners. In this new atmosphere, Charlotte's marriage to Albert would hardly have been an impediment to leaving him and marrying Werther; and Paul would not have wasted away mourning a Virginia who refused to take off her clothes. The fantasy that, "if I truly loved, I'd be obsessed with him/her," or "if he/she truly loved me, he/she'd be obsessed with me" might seem a relic of the past.

Yet breakups of romantic relationships are a well-known flash point for suicide attempts. While not couched in the passionate language of Goethe, a recent study suggests that the more committed and invested partners are in a romantic relationship, the more likely they are to sink into depression and attempt suicide when the relationship founders.[38] Some scientists specializing in brain chemistry liken intense romantic love to substance abuse: both are addictive, and both engage the reward pathways of the brain. "Most characteristic, the lover thinks obsessively about the beloved."[39] These scientists are focused on therapies for love addiction; they turn out to be similar to the remedies offered by Galen some two thousand years ago: diversions such as staying busy, exercising, finding a hobby, and so on. But if some people do not seek cures – Bess Gornick lying on her couch, Werther obsessing in his letters, Bernart de Ventadorn rejoicing in his pain, Penelope shedding tears for twenty years – let us note that there may be a method to their madness: the reward system of the brain.

In a *New Yorker* short story by Kate Folk, "Out There," the narrator is looking for a romantic partner.[40] She tries some online dating apps, but fears finding not only a creep but a "blot" – a robot that is a tactile illusion: he looks like a handsome man, is charming and empathetic and sexually adept – and disappears in a puff of smoke once he has taken a woman's personal information. Blots are employed by a company in Russia "to target vulnerable women." Our narrator is delighted when Sam, a man she matches with on Tinder, has some obvious flaws. He is not perfectly handsome, not very empathetic or charming, and not particularly good at sex. Wonderful! But after some very boring months with Sam, the narrator breaks it off. He may not be a blot, but he's not the love of her life.

A bit later, walking in Golden Gate Park, she sees "five identical men" at a picnic table. One of them spots her and begins a charming, flattering spiel. She gratefully joins him at the table. Better a perfect blot who will be like Paul or Werther – attending to her every need – than a real man. Even if he will soon disappear in a puff of smoke once he has all her information. For our narrator, the illusion of obsessive love is better than the love that real people can give. Maybe it was that way for Penelope too.

5

Insatiability

The original aim of Plato's *Symposium* was to praise the god of love. But two speeches challenged that goal's very premise. Pausanias, speaking early in the evening, declared that there were *two* gods of love, one inferior to the other. Then, toward the end of the evening, Socrates presented Diotima's subversive view that Eros was not a god at all. Both relied on different myths of love's origin.

There's no doubt, said Pausanias, that Eros is Aphrodite's partner, but there are two goddesses of that name, one born of a male god alone, the other the daughter of a god and a water nymph. The Eros that is the consort of that second, "common" Aphrodite is, therefore, inferior to the Eros who accompanies the god-born, "heavenly" Aphrodite. The common sort of love "strikes wherever he gets a chance." He's not particular: men, women, boys – they're all just fine. Moreover, he is insatiable. Those inspired by him care about nothing but "completing the sexual act" (181b).[1] They don't care how or why they do it; they simply attach themselves to anyone coming their way. Pausanias was morally outraged by this form of love, and in the course of his speech he advocated laws against its excesses.

Diotima was not at the party, so she couldn't dispute Pausanias directly. But had she been there, she surely would have done so, for Diotima maintained that there was one Eros. He was neither common nor heavenly but the mixture and offspring of two daemons: Need (his mother) and Resourcefulness (his father). Yes, he was the consort of the goddess Aphrodite, but only because he had been conceived at her birthday party. His conception was happenstance: Resourcefulness had been a guest at the celebration, got drunk, wandered away, and fell asleep. Need, begging at the gate, saw her chance to get something, lay with Resourcefulness, and got pregnant with Love. Like his mother, Diotima explained, Love is dirty and shoeless, always looking for the main chance, always wanting, needing, and desiring. At the same time, like his father, "he is brave, impetuous, and intense, an awesome hunter, always weaving snares, resourceful in his pursuit of intelligence, a lover of wisdom through all his life, a genius with enchantments, potions, and clever pleadings" (203d). Eros is not wise, beautiful, and virtuous, as the gods are, but he is smart enough to want all those attributes and does all he can to get them. Yet he is always disappointed, for he can never quite have his way. Then he dies, but soon he springs back to life. He's no god, but neither is he mortal; he's something in between.

This is Diotima's jaundiced vision of love – all love – and so it is no wonder that she quickly leaves behind the transient joy of loving another person. Instead, she uses love's propelling and insatiable desire to possess, along with its inexhaustible bag of tricks to get what it wants, to take the lover up the ladder that leads from bodies to souls to laws and ideas and, finally, at last, to the ravishment of eternal beauty, truth, and virtue.

But if Diotima *had* left Eros on the first rung, eager to make his way from body to body, he would have been a lot like Pausanias' "common love," though much smarter, more cunning, and, in a word, more seductive – a flirt ready to hit on everyone in sight.

Love as insatiability is the least sentimental of the fantasies featured in this book, and some readers will want to ask: is it really love? Isn't it just lust?

But "lust" is itself a fantasy of *not*-love created largely by churchmen to decry sexual desire in general – unless turned to the uses God had originally intended for it. To denote the sin of lust, the Church narrowed the meaning of the Latin word *luxuria*, which had originally covered every sort of excess, not only or even mainly the erotic sort. When Pope Gregory the Great named the seven deadly sins on the tree of vices, he put *luxuria* at the top, right above gluttony. Those were the two "carnal vices," he said; gluttony was connected to the belly, lust to the genitals.[2] Although, as we saw in chapter 2, Origen was sure that the biblical Song of Songs was talking about a spiritual ladder of love, he worried that another reader, still mired in "his bodily nature," might think that "Divine Scriptures . . . are thus urging and egging him on to fleshly lust!"[3] He warned people like that not to read the Song. In the twelfth century, when theologians were turning married love into a divine sacrament and therefore something wonderful, apart from the sex (see chapter 3), they excluded all other forms of carnal love as sinful fornication.

It is true that the ancient world, too, had notions of unbridled Eros, as I discuss briefly below. Fitting into that ancient view was Pausanias' disapproval of "common love." But he didn't say it was not love at all, just that it was an inferior form. Diotima belittled all forms of love that dwelled on bodies. On the other hand, drawing out the implications of her argument that love is a combination of neediness and cunning, she might have admitted that insatiable love is indeed a manifestation of Eros, but one that flits from one first rung to another. The flirting among the men at the *Symposium* was just background noise in that dialogue, but, had it been foregrounded, it might have sounded like praise of Eros' endless cruising.

There is, moreover, another argument in favor of giving insatiability the recognition it craves as love: its language is exactly the same as – if more frank, raunchy, and irreverent than – all the other forms of love. It declares itself to be love. Of course, one might object that it lies, and that such lies are part of its wheedling manipulation. But I would answer that Diotima was right here: *all* the fantasies of love involve some posing, dissembling, and embellishing to one degree or another – whether to oneself or to the beloved. Think of Odysseus not telling Penelope about his amorous liaisons before he got home; think of her not telling him about the time she descended to the great hall to turn all her suitors' knees to water.

Sexual disporting in the ancient world

Pausanias was arguably right to separate out two kinds of love, but they certainly mingled together in the Greek world of his time. Upstanding families showed off vases decorated with black and red figures of men penetrating and spanking women or showing satyrs huge of penis as they pursue maenads in the forest. Ancient Greeks considered these images to be transgressive and hilarious. Satyrs had outsize penises, but the Greek masculine ideal was a small penis, neat and compact.

At Rome, Augustus tried to legislate fidelity and sex for procreation only, but terracotta workshops of his era knew better, churning out cups decorated with elegant men and women coupling in a tantalizing variety of positions. Upper-class consumers bought more refined depictions of the same poses on luxury items (see figure 12). Romans living at Pompeii decorated their rooms – even those meant for public receptions – with couples disporting in idyllic settings. Brothels gussied up cubicles meant for quick sex with languorous images of endless love-making.

In the ancient world (as in some places today), phalluses were thought to ward off danger and evil. Many a respectable shop, bath, and tomb made strategic use of phallic images to ensure their protection. This was not pornography in the modern sense. Nor were the erotic scenes that decorated the wine jugs used by Roman soldiers stationed along the River Rhône. There was nothing furtive here; sex and genitals were there for all to see and enjoy.

Much of this changed under the impress of Christianity. But we have already seen that insatiable love was well known to the pupils (male and female) who read Ovid in medieval schools. The marginal illustration in figure 10 and the obscene verses of fabliaux make clear that unbridled sex was a frequent (and well-skewered) topic in the medieval period. It could even be the fodder of ditties, as in the verses of a troubadour known as "Tribolet":

A fucker who was not in love
With any girl, but wanted to fuck
Always had a hard-on, and was eager
To fuck any woman he could fuck.

The poet denies that the fucker was in love. But that's not what the fucker says:

And he said, "He lives badly who doesn't fuck
Night and day the one he loves."[4]

Around the same time as Tribolet was writing, King James I of Aragon (d. 1276) had three wives and at least three mistresses and loved them all, if the records of his gifts are any indication, for he called one wife "beloved" and "dearest," while all his ladies were "beloved."[5]

Mining official royal acts for words of love, however, is rather like plowing rocky soil with a stick. Plenty of medieval men left their wives for greener pastures, and some local customary laws explicitly gave them permission to do so. But it is hard to know what love had to do with it. There simply isn't much evidence one way or another of insatiable Pausanian love. For that, we must turn to the early modern period.

Roving hands

Writing around 1600, John Donne likened his mistress to the New World, his hands to the eager explorers of colonial delights:

> License my roving hands, and let them go,
> Before, behind, between, above, below.
> O my America! my new-found-land.[6]

Himself a member of Raleigh's expedition to Guyana, Donne no doubt agreed that the New World was "a country that has yet her maidenhead: never sacked, turned, nor wrought [quarried]."[7] She was ripe for the taking. In a sixteenth-century image of Amerigo Vespucci's landing in America, the continent is personified as a voluptuous female, nearly naked, roused in surprise from her repose (see figure 13). She signals her welcome to the explorer, who meets her startled look with a steady gaze, his feet firmly planted on the ground, his body well protected by armor. Holding an astrolabe with one hand, a symbol of Europe's scientific advancement, with the other he plants a flag decorated with a cross. The image announces Europe's superiority in every way: male, invulnerable, and Christian. Vespucci is the conquering hero ready to "take" the woman, master the animals that now roam freely in the unruly wilderness, and extinguish the fire (tended by the natives behind her) that is here roasting human flesh.

The triumphant conquest of "virgin" territory by Europeans begins to explain why Renaissance artists, humanists, and poets looked at ancient erotic representations in a new way. The Renaissance didn't "discover" classical antiquity – that had always been there, in books, frescoes, and statues long appreciated during the Middle Ages. But new preoccupations led to repurposing the past. Inspired by some engravings depicting various "sex positions" reminiscent of Pompeiian wall paintings, Pietro Aretino (d. 1556) wrote accompanying sonnets. While Petrarch had made sonnets a way to express enduring love; Aretino made them transgressive:

Open your thighs so I can look straight
  At your beautiful ass and cunt in my face,
  An ass equal to paradise in its enjoyment,
  A cunt that melts hearts through the kidneys.

While I compare these things,
  Suddenly I long to kiss you,
  And I seem to myself more handsome than Narcissus
  In the mirror that keeps my prick erect.[8]

This was the upside-down world of the Venetian carnival, transferred from the streets into poetry and thus doubly scandalous. Aretino thumbed his nose at the Church and respectability, affirming the "naturalness" of erotic representation. In a letter to a friend, he declared: "I reject the furtive attitude and filthy custom that forbid the eyes what delights them most." He wanted to celebrate the penis, "the thing which is given to us by nature to preserve the race." It "should be worn around the neck as a pendant, or pinned onto the cap like a broach."[9] Around the time he was writing this letter, he was also commissioning a bronze medallion that featured on the obverse his portrait and on the reverse his personal emblem: the head of a satyr, composed entirely of pricks and balls (see figure 14).

In Aretino's *Dialogues*, another daring work, a courtesan named Nanna discusses the future she should arrange for her daughter, Pippa. Should Pippa become a nun, a wife, or a whore? Nanna's friend Antonia thinks the decision should not be hard, since Nanna has practiced all these professions in turn. As it turns out, they hardly differ: all are empires of roving hands. Thus, in the nunnery, and right away, Nanna loses her virginity, takes a fleet of lovers, watches orgies through the cracks in the walls of her cell, and discovers the erotic uses of every bodily orifice. In short, she disports like a maenad in the forests and mountains of Aretino's imagination. After a jealous lover nearly skins her alive, she has her mother save her from her cloistered "tranquility" and is soon settled with a husband. But little changes, for husbands are hardly satisfying and so every wife must take lovers. Nanna and Antonia have great fun talking about the "pious" wives who amuse themselves with their priestly, eremitic, and monastic swains. One lover boasts a "yard-long white staff with a reddish tip," another a "smoking stool-leg with its fiery, burning tip and its length all dotted with warts."[10] As for courtesans, why, they enjoy the same pleasures and make money to boot. It's settled: Pippa must become a whore.

Aretino was mocking the society of his day: plenty of Italian families put their daughters into undisciplined convents, whether because they could not pay for a dowry or because it counted as a pious thing to do. Similarly, many fathers and mothers married their daughters off to men like Nanna's fictive husband: rich, old, and alive only "because he was eating." Some women did indeed ply the trade of prostitute or courtesan, and at times they wedded one of their lovers. With individual exceptions – in art and music, for example, and also (in the popular imagination) witchcraft – there were few other professions for women in Italy at this time. Nanna and Antonia were talking about reality, although with the exaggerations permitted by satire.

But were they talking about love? Yes, indeed, claimed Aretino: Nanna was revealing what love really is. The sex in the *Dialogues* is accompanied by all the phrases of love coined by the love poets: sweet words of endearment ("my soul of souls, my heart of hearts, my life of lives," declares one smitten lover ready to pounce), passionate jealousy, quotations from poetry, and the very words love (*amore*) and lovers (*amanti*). And there are offspring as well, for, as an ersatz friar teaches the nuns, nature "delights in seeing her creatures increase and multiply." Of a whore's love, Nanna explains: "Her love is like a termite's: the more it gets to gnaw at, the more the thing becomes dear to it." This is the way the world works.

Aretino promoted, enjoyed, laughed at, and skewered insatiable love, the love that the courtesan satisfies. Her life, he declared, is "divine" because it is the least hypocritical of all. That was a poke at pious warnings about avarice. For Aretino, the best kind of life takes its money along with its pleasures. He knew about getting rich; his books were on the Index of Prohibited Books and even so (or therefore?) were read by an avid and international reading public. Aretino understood, as did only a few others in his day, how to take advantage of the heady "start-up" known as the printing press. He freed himself from the tyranny of patrons by profiting from his best-sellers. His most popular book was his letter collection – his own letters, daringly published during his own lifetime. They bore witness to his wide social network and made him into one of the world's first "influencers." Titian, his close friend, painted his portrait several times and once used him as his model for the figure of Pontius Pilate. He was a famous man by the end of his life: the reverse of a medallion then created in his honor depicted him not as a satyr but as an impresario, seated on a throne as four princes in antique dress, heads bowed, offer him tribute.

Even as he ratified the ancient prejudice that women's sexual appetites were ravenous, Aretino gave women a certain agency. Indeed, they ran the show by acting the part – the male fantasy – of the pure, compliant, willing maiden. Nanna tells Pippa how to feign femininity with her lover, even when he is old and ugly, even as he stinks and farts: she must first sigh and blush, for those "are the signs of love and set the passion hammers throbbing." She must behave like the wife in *The Good Wife's Guide* (see chapter 3), except that in bed she must pretend to delight in her companion's love-making. It's all pretense, and she will make good money. On the other hand, it's a hard job: the onus of maintaining the fantasy is on her. Aretino pokes fun at the gullible men who fall for the lie, but he is mainly writing *for* them, offering them the simulacrum of a love that exists to fulfill their needs.

A century later, the tradition begun by Aretino was burgeoning. Books dedicated to titillating while ostensibly teaching men and women how to service insatiable love – their own and others' – proliferated. In France came (for example) *The Academy of Ladies* (*L'Académie des dames*) and *The Girls' School, or the Philosophy of Ladies* (*L'Ecole des filles, ou la philosophie des dames*) (1655). The latter was translated into English as *The School of Venus*. The English version featured a frontispiece of three ladies happily surveying the penises they might buy from a female purveyor. Inside were numerous illustrations of many of the possible "fucking postures."[11] The story of *The School of Venus*, such as it is, involves a compact between Roger, in love with naive young Katy, and Frances, Katy's worldly-wise cousin. Following through with her part of the agreement, Frances instructs the clueless girl in how "one half of the world fucks the other." Everyone does it; nothing is out of bounds. The knowing lady names – and renames, and names again with all the vulgar terms she can muster – the body parts involved in sex. She describes the nature of foreplay, expounds on the positions of intercourse, and praises the pleasures so graphically that Katy has "a great mind to be trying the sport." And so she does, happily describing to Frances (in the second half of the book) her adventures with Roger. Pamphlets such as *The School of Venus* were the stalking horses for novels.

Writings like these were subversive and were treated as such. The putative authors of *The School of Venus* were brought to trial and punished. Their book advanced a radical argument: as Frances opined, "I cannot think lechery a sin; I am sure if women governed the world and the Church as men do, you would soon find they would account fucking so lawful that it would not be accounted a misdemeanor." The only reason that men call it a sin, she continued, is "for fear of giving too much liberty to the women." Such ideas laughed at pious traditions. At the same time, they fit well with the new science of the seventeenth century, when Newton, Galileo, and others turned disparate bodies into abstract "masses," each exerting a force on the other, uninhibited unless acted upon by yet another object. So, too, men and women were equal in attracting one another, a fact that led inexorably to the push and pull, the in and out, of sex. Love's needs were as natural as the earth circling the sun.

Or, rather, as natural as smooth balls rolling forever on an absolutely featureless surface. For, even as they came together in sex, the lovers of *The School* were disconnected from ordinary life and context. Though the business of *The School* takes place in a vaguely upper-class setting, with a maid puttering about, its protagonists exist mainly as sex machines, unmoored from kinship networks, churches, and neighborhoods.

They make their own way in the world, acting according to what the materialist philosopher Thomas Hobbes (d. 1679), writing around the same time, called their "imagination" and "passion." Frances' attitude towards pregnancy suggests the extreme atomization involved: hide your belly until near the end of your term, then go to the countryside, have the baby, and leave it there. Better yet, get married so that any children you may have will be thought your husband's – whether they are or not. This was almost surely the fantasy of a male author.

Indeed, the (almost always) anonymous authors of this sort of literature were probably men. Even so, a perusal of Paris police records from the period reveals that, at least in France, women were deeply involved in the production and distribution of such books.[12] Moreover, the voices we hear in them are those of women. Although their stories surely titillated male audiences, and although they featured phallic-centered pleasures, the women were the heroines. Male fantasies though they were, they nevertheless shattered the strictures of Christian morality as surely as Copernicus had defied the earth-centered beliefs of his day. Some of these heroines, less prim than the cousins in *The School*, even reported on the joys that men had when coupling with men, women with women, and occasionally all in combination together.

*

In the eighteenth century, the exploration of inner thoughts and subjective feeling was taken to a new level in novels. Like many others of the genre, Samuel Richardson's *Pamela, or Virtue Rewarded* (1740), used the immediacy of letters to transport readers into the minds of the protagonists through identification, empathy, and imagination. *Pamela* was a sort of English Protestant saint's life, harking back to numerous Catholic female (and sometimes male) holy people beset by attempted seductions. What was new in *Pamela* was that lust (on the part of the man) and repulsion (on the part of the woman) turned into love and marriage.

Richardson's long book is about the poor but beautiful servant Pamela and her Houdini-like escapes from the attempts at rape of her "master," Mr. B., a "gentleman of pleasure and intrigue."[13] In the end, she realizes that she loves him (and he realizes he loves her in turn), and they marry. And only then do they have sex (though readers must imagine their wedding night). But the fact that her husband soon gives her forty-eight rules for good wifely behavior, including one demanding that she "be flexible as the reed in the fable, lest, by resisting the tempest, like the oak, [she] be torn up by the roots," suggests that he might continue to try to "rape" her even after their marriage. I put rape in quotation marks because English law at the time expressly denied the possibility of "marital rape": the husband always had the right to have sex with his wife, with or without her consent. This remained the law in England and Wales until the 1990s and part of America's common law legacy until the 1970s.[14]

Pamela was an immediate best-seller and also a target of criticism and satire. Perhaps the most cutting was Henry Fielding's *Shamela*, whose heroine, daughter of a prostitute, is a lascivious schemer who tricks her unwitting master into marrying her. But by far the most popular and enduring "answer" to *Pamela* was John Cleland's *Memoirs of a Woman of Pleasure*, better known as *Fanny Hill* (1748–9). In her whoring, Fanny was a bit like Nanna; in her ecstatic enjoyment of sex, a lot like Katy. She was also like Pamela in marrying the man she loved in the end.

Written while Cleland was imprisoned for debt, *Memoirs* was his first book, and it forever hounded his serious literary ambitions and the reception of his many other writings. To be sure, it sold out and went through many clandestine editions and translations, but it was banned in the United States until 1963 and in England until 1970. Its detailed, rapturous descriptions of Fanny's delicious sensual pleasures, together with its brief glimpse of two men having sex together, obscured for most readers its serious argument: sensual experimentation for both men and women is an excellent prelude to both true love and virtue. Put another way, insatiable love may pave the way to monogamy.

Cleland drew on the newest thought of his era. In *An Essay Concerning Human Understanding*, John Locke (d. 1704) argued that we are not born with innate ideas implanted in us either by God or by nature. Rather, we gain everything we know through our senses alone. Experience is the key. Of course, some of us merely stick to our simple ideas and a few easy associations, such as Locke's universal "I love whatever gives me pleasure,"[15] or a few habitual and ingrained notions such as "My mother told me that virginity is virtuous, so it must be virtuous." But other people, superior people, reflect on their ideas and associations and reformulate them in accordance with still other reflections.

Fanny reflected on a topic that Locke never discussed: sex. Odd, perhaps, that he omitted it, for sex was the focal sense experience of *The School of Venus* and other literature of the sort. Had Locke lived to read *Pamela*, and had he been moved to comment on her behavior, he might have observed that a moral rule such as "hold onto thy virginity" came to Pamela from habit alone. For, given her inexperience, how could she possibly know what sex was about or whether it was a good or bad thing? And, given Locke's universal pleasure principle, how could she have "fallen in love" with a man who had given her only pain?

Fanny, unlike Pamela, experiences every sort of sex imaginable. She must: her chief sense organ is her "soft laboratory of love," in which, like a good scientist, she does her experiments.[16] It is true that Cleland is less brave than Aretino: he has a continuum of love, at the top of which is "true love," the love that Fanny feels for Charles, the handsome young man with whom she loses her virginity. But, like Voltaire's Candide, whose story was published ten years after Fanny's, she is rudely banished from her idyll when Charles is sent off to the South Seas. By fending for herself in a world of good, bad, and indifferent humanity, she comes to wisdom.

The body knows more than the mind. When, before meeting Charles, Fanny is initiated into sexual touching by the other girls at Mrs. Brown's brothel, she is "transported, confused, and out of myself." A young innocent with hardly an idea yet formed (she is a virgin of fifteen), she doesn't know what to make of her sensations; she has no "liberty of thought." But the "frolic and thoughtless gaiety" of the other girls and the glimpses of sex she sees in the house inflame her "principle of pleasure." Since she has only the habits she was brought up with rather than well-considered reflections, her morals soon descend to those of her house-mates. She is curious when she hears noises in an adjacent room and then mesmerized when she sees through a peephole a man unbuttoning his pants and producing, "naked, stiff, and erect, that wonderful machine." The sight stirs up her "seat of pleasure." She knows by "the instinct of nature" that from that stiff "machine" she "was to expect that supreme pleasure which [nature] has placed in the meeting of those parts so admirably fitted for each other."

That "admirable fit" was among the numerous lessons that Fanny learned, though many other forms of sexual knowledge were helpful in forming her human understanding. Consider masturbation, that "self-viewing, self-touching, self-enjoying, *in fine* . . . all the means of *self-knowledge*." It was self-gratifying love at its most extreme, though not at its best. Beyond that were all possible experiences with men. But there was one form of knowledge that Fanny (and probably Cleland) condemned: sex between men. Fanny called it "criminal," reflecting the new prohibitions against "sodomy" adopted in England in the eighteenth century. (The word "homosexuality" was invented only at the end of the nineteenth.) But even though she decried it, Fanny described in great detail the one homosexual encounter that she saw; only by experiencing it vicariously could her readers reflect on its wrongness. How ironic that Cleland himself was accused of such relations!

But let us return to the many moments when "the parts" of the man and the woman fit together properly. In that case, sex is pure bliss. It is best when the two pleasure-seekers are beautiful, the woman as lovely as Fanny herself, the man a "hunk" – or, as Fanny puts it, "as pretty a piece of woman's meat as you should see." Beautiful people get fired up and have joy from one another more exquisite than the ordinary "pleasure merely animal" of "the collisions of the sexes by a passive bodily effect." And when, like the young Will whom Fanny seduces (rejoicing at her power to produce his enormous erection), the man is also appealing in personality, Fanny speaks of love. Cleland tries, then, to distinguish animal sex from love sex, and love sex from true love. Will is not Fanny's true love. With Will is none of "that sweet fury, that rage of active delight which crowns the enjoyments of a mutual love-passion, where two hearts tenderly and truly united, club to exalt the joy." "Club" seems an odd word here, but not in the context of Cleland's eighteenth century, when it referred to a mutual society. Here too was an echo of Locke, in this case of his *Two Treatises of Government*, where he stressed man's sociability, his need and desire to club together with others.

When Charles returns from his long sea voyage, his reunion with Fanny is as passionate as that of Odysseus and Penelope. And yet Fanny has not spent the interval weeping. "All the better," is Cleland's implicit response. Only through sex – through reflecting on and comparing her experiences of the "truth! stark naked truth" – has Fanny been able to see *why* her life of insatiable love had been "scandalous." Only then does she deserve "every blessing in the power of love, health, and fortune to bestow." Those blessings include marriage and children, Cleland's coming to terms with social mores.

Fanny's life was rarely read because it illustrated Lockean principles; it was read because it was shocking and pleasurable, and because it argued (at least superficially) for the sort of love that Pausanias had labeled inferior. On both those points, it was part of a larger eighteenth-century literature of sexual manipulators, miscreants, and libertines who challenged religious sensibilities, the hypocrisy of social relations among the upper classes, and the pretense of sexual fidelity.

Apart from Cleland's *Memoirs*, however, most of this literature denigrated rather than celebrated insatiable love's endless duplicity. Thus, in Choderlos de Laclos' *Dangerous Liaisons* (1782), the plotting protagonists, the Vicomte de Valmont and the Marquise de Merteuil, carefully distinguish between sex and love. Love they disdain: only fools fall in love. Nevertheless, for their purposes they have mastered all the "parasitical" words and phrases of love – straight out of the playbook of the amorous medieval poets.[17] Armed with that verbal and gestural toolkit of tears, sighs, and professions of endless passion, they pry open and play upon the emotional tinderbox lying within their victims. To the beautiful and virtuous Mme de Tourvel, the new object of his sensual desires, Valmont writes: "The very table on which I am writing, dedicated for the first time to this use, has become for me the sacred altar of love." That "table" is in fact the rump of his accommodating female companion of the moment. Laclos here paints a tableau of aristocratic dissipation and immorality that helped pave the road to the French Revolution.

But there is more to the story than satire. Every reader immediately realizes that the truly important relationship in this novel is between Valmont and Merteuil, the two manipulators, even though they would have laughed off the suggestion. It is clear, too, that Valmont is not the only one playing with ideas of love; Mme de Tourvel, who (at first) resists all his advances and shreds one of his ardent letters in front of his eyes, is (privately) powerfully moved by her ability to inspire such passion in another. Without quite knowing why, she pastes together the torn letter and wets it with her tears. Both she and her seducer revel in their ability to inspire love in another. "License my roving hands," wrote Donne; the very declaration of love is a form of power over others, even as it pretends to be submission.

The language of war and the hunt is the lingo of love as well. Valmont has dedicated his life to making beautiful women his prey; he desires nothing more than to drag out his wooing so that his quarry will give up her virtue only after "a long-drawn-out agony." For her part, Merteuil claims that she has entirely mastered the art of pretending to be in love. Like Fanny, she has made careful observations and "thought long and hard." Unlike Fanny, she has focused not on her sensations but, rather, on what the men and women in high society "were trying to hide." From her observations, she learns to "dissemble," to mask her feelings and use their opposite in her gestures and expressions. She figures out how to inspire love precisely by not feeling it, by retreating behind a veil of virtue and prudery when in reality she is advancing into a whirlwind of amusement and pleasure. "Have you not," she writes to Valmont, "come to the conclusion that [I was] born to avenge my sex and conquer yours?"

These people think they have all of love's crafty resourcefulness and none of its neediness. They are fooling themselves. Need wins out when Valmont falls in love with Mme de Tourvel; it wins again when Merteuil cannot suppress her terrible jealousy. But Laclos wants to unmask more than the emotional weaknesses of his protagonists. He wants to expose their conformity to society's demands even as they imagine themselves to be free. Thus, when Merteuil demands that Valmont break off all contact with Mme de Tourvel, he does so because he fears social ridicule, the accusation that he had "a romantic and unhappy love affair." His reputation is all. Merteuil puts her finger on it: "You would have sacrificed a thousand more [women] rather than be laughed at." Twenty years before Laclos published *Liaisons*, Rousseau's *Social Contract* argued that men (and women) were born free but were everywhere in chains, fettered by social conventions. Laclos agreed: Merteuil and Valmont thought they had kicked over the traces; in fact, they were utterly in harness.

Lovers in motion

All the protagonists and their victims in *Dangerous Liaisons* suffer in the end. That, indeed, was the fate of most of the fictional libertines of the eighteenth century, though not until they had reaped more than their fair share of pleasure and wreaked havoc on the lives of others. The Enlightenment justified – and social changes encouraged – the emergence of a newly sexualized culture not just among the aristocracy, so bitterly depicted by Laclos, but also among the bourgeoisie. Rather than empowering women, as the "emancipated" Merteuil seems to have hoped, the new eroticism subjected them to even greater sexual control by men. The influential philosopher Immanuel Kant (d. 1804) theorized the nature of woman as morally and intellectually deficient. Her "beautiful soul" needed to be (as he put it) "curated" by her husband. Eighteenth-century women's journals (much like blogs, social media, and women's magazines today) pitched to a newly literate middle-class female readership the desirability of a beautiful face and body to attract and keep a man.

All this encouraged a literature of seduction, initially condemned (as in *Dangerous Liaisons*) but gradually celebrated as well. The Marquis de Sade (d. 1814) was utterly unrepentant about his own dissolute life, and he trumpeted "vice" (which he considered virtuous) in his fiction. Claiming the status of a *philosophe*, he made Nature his guide:

> To Libertines of all ages, and of every sex, and of every inclination, it is you to whom I dedicate this work. Your passions, which the cold and dreary moralists tell you to fear, are nothing more than the means by which Nature seeks to exhort you to do Her work. . . . Young virgins, . . . throw off the restraints of your ridiculous religion, spurn the precepts of your idiotic parents; yield, instead, to the laws of Nature which logic describes, and to the arms of those who would be your lovers. Lascivious men: . . . acknowledge no government save that of your desires, no limits save those of your imagination.[18]

Life is woeful; we never asked to be born; the best we can do is snatch pleasure wherever possible.

A chronology of Sade's life in a scholarly edition of his works reads like a litany of sins: at the age of nineteen, he already had "a reputation for lewd conduct"; thereafter, he seduced women and men, enjoyed sado-masochistic encounters, and exulted in "horrible impiety" – desecrating a crucifix, for example. In just one year, 1771 (he was thirty-one), his wife gave birth to their third child, he was imprisoned for debt, and he seduced his wife's sister. In 1772, he, his valet, and four prostitutes partied. One of the women fell ill from an aphrodisiac, and, to escape the law, Sade and his infatuated sister-in-law fled to Italy, where he was arrested and jailed. He found time to write by churning out tracts, plays, and novels during his many stints in prison.[19] Was any of this about love? All of it, Sade would have answered. Listen to the opening dialogue of *Philosophy in the Bedroom*:

> *Scene: Saint-Ange's bedroom. She lies on bed, clad only in a nightgown. There is a rap on the door. Enter, the Horseman [her brother].*
> SAINT-ANGE: A good afternoon to you, Horseman.
>   Where, pray tell, is your friend, Dolmancé?
> HORSEMAN: He'll be here presently, my love. I trust you
>   can keep rein on your passions for an hour or two.
>   If not, spread your sweet thighs and permit me to
>   serve you.[20]

"My love," "your sweet thighs," pledges of service: these were and remain part and parcel of the language of love in the West.

The careers of Faust and Don Juan began with moral condemnation, but by the end of the eighteenth century they drew admiration. The story of Faust, originally (in its sixteenth-century German version) a magician and (above all) a non-believer, morphed into the tale of a womanizer who sells his soul to the devil and (as it played out in the writings of the German poet Goethe [d. 1832]) was lauded for doing so. The tale circulated throughout Europe, and as a child Goethe no doubt saw it in the form of a traveling puppet show. It preoccupied him throughout his life. In his earliest version, the so-called *Urfaust* (1770s), Goethe condemned the pleasure-seeking hero who seduced and abandoned the innocent Margareta. (This was around the same time as he published *The Sorrows of Young Werther*.)

But in his final version of the Faust story he saved his hero, praising Faust's womanizing as the foundation of his "restless striving." What matters most in life is male insatiability – in love and war, in accumulating property and power. Nothing is ever enough. A restless spirit cannot abide stability. And so, after Faust's affair with Margareta and a blissful tryst with Helen of Troy, he becomes a successful nineteenth-century entrepreneur, clearing land, building dikes, and ruthlessly mowing down all who stand in his way. Lust is here paired with avarice, and both are virtues. Faust dismisses any anxious doubts about his way of life as "phantoms":

> Press on regardless – but let him remain
> Dissatisfied each moment of the day! (11451–2)[21]

When Faust dies, heavenly angels cheat the Devil of his due, and, as they carry the hero's soul to the empyrean realms, they explain:

> This noble spirit is released
> From evil and damnation;
> *For those whose striving never ceased*
> *We can lead to salvation.* (11934–7)

Goethe gave those last words italicized emphasis. Did they mean Faust was saved *in spite of* all his sins? Not at all. He was saved because of them. Margareta, the seduced and abandoned woman, now a penitent in heaven, is delighted, crying out to Mary, the "glorious mother,"

> Matchless in grace,
> Our Lady incline
> Your radiant face
> Upon this happiness of mine!
> My lover – see,
> Transfigured, he
> Returns to me! (12069–75)

Will he remain true to her in heaven? One may doubt it. For, at the very end of this long, versified drama, as if to sum up its moral, the mystical choir declares,

What is not understood,
Here it is done;
Eternal womanhood
Draws us all on. (12108–11)

Eternal womanhood, *das Ewig-Weibliche*: Margareta and Helen simply embody the magnetic pole that draws men to accomplish great things. The Faust legend began with condemning Pausanias' inferior Eros; it ended by granting it a halo.

*

That was, in outline, the happy fate of Don Juan as well. Originally, in the play by Tirso de Molina, published in 1630, Juan is a trickster who ravishes and destroys every woman he meets. At Naples he disguises himself as the lover of a duchess in order to get into her bed. Later he washes up on the shores of Spain to find safety in the arms of Thisbe, a fisherman's daughter: "Noble young man, so handsome, gay, / And exquisite, wake up, I say!"[22]

He promises her his love forever, and, before they make love, she reminds him that "God exists – and death." But, carefree as the wind, he has already had the horses saddled to get away as soon as he has bedded her; and he has given orders to burn down poor Thisbe's hut to divert attention from his escape. In this fashion, Don Juan seduces his way through Spain, women falling at his feet. But his pleasure is not so much in satisfying needy love as in deceiving. As he confesses:

> . . . In Seville
> I'm called the Trickster; and my greatest pleasure
> Is to trick women, leaving them dishonored.

Recalling Diotima's vocabulary, we may say that Juan's insatiability is due less to Need than to delight in his Resourcefulness. But, in one trick too many, he kills

Don Gonzalo, the father of his near conquest Doña Ana (who discovers his disguise before it succeeds). Later, the stone statue of Gonzalo plays its own trick, inviting Juan to dine with it in an empty tomb. At the end of a meal of snakes, vinegar, fingernails, and ice, the statue offers its hand, and, as Juan grasps it, he feels the fire of Hell. He begs to be absolved by a priest, but the statue says it is too late, and Juan falls dead.

But soon, as in Molière's play *Don Juan* of 1665, Juan *refuses* to repent: "No, no, it will never be said, whatever happens, that I repented."[23] He cares about keeping his posthumous reputation as a womanizer. Delight in that life is even clearer in the opera *Don Giovanni* (1787) by Mozart and his librettist da Ponte, when Giovanni's seductions are so charmingly portrayed in music and verse that one can hardly blame Zerlina, the peasant girl whom he woos, for giving in to his pleas:

DON GIOVANNI. Come! Come!
        There you will give me your hand.
    ZERLINA. Soon I won't be able to resist.[24]

Nor can Donna Elvira, already once seduced and abandoned by him, give up her hopes of getting him back:

DONNA ELVIRA: . . . Can I believe that my tears have
    won over
        your heart? That, penitent, my beloved Don
        Giovanni returns to his duty and to my love?

She had better not believe it; Giovanni cannot live without the insatiable love that Pausanius and the marriage sacrament and most of society decried: "Love is much the same in any form. He who / remains faithful to one [woman] is being cruel to the others." This Mozartian Don Juan refuses to repent ten times over.

Thus, by the time Lord Byron (d. 1824) took up the theme, Don Juan had become a romantic hero, free not so much because a nobleman might play tricks on ladies but above all because this Don, this lord, this man, was true to himself. Byron's Juan is an exceedingly attractive young fellow and resourceful as well. Caught *in flagrante* with his first love, he must wander over land and sea. Like Odysseus, he is shipwrecked on a Grecian shore and nursed back to health by a beautiful young woman, Haidee. Like another Nausicaa, she falls in love with him. But, rejecting the model of Homer, Juan does not meet her invitation with pious words about the like-minded-ness that makes for a good marriage. To the contrary, he and Haidee live the fantasy life that all of Penelope's suitors dreamt of. While Haidee's father, Lambro, is off to sea, plundering and enslaving other lands and people, the two young lovers feast at Lambro's expense, enjoying the infinite pleasures of mutual passion:

> She loved, and was beloved – she adored,
>   And she was worshipp'd; after nature's fashion,
> Their intense souls, into each other pour'd. (2.191)[25]

"After nature's fashion": love is natural. So, too, is falling in love many times, very often, and with different people. It is a fact of the human condition. Nothing squelches love better than marriage, and this is true for both sexes. Women are by nature fickle: "Whether wed, / Or widow, maid, or mother, she can change her / Mind like the wind" (9.64). And men are not much different, try as they might to be:

> I hate inconstancy – I loathe, detest,
>   Abhor, condemn, abjure the mortal made
> Of such quicksilver clay that in his breast
>   No permanent foundation can be laid;
> Love, constant love, has been my constant guest,
>   And yet last night, being at a masquerade,
> I saw the prettiest creature, fresh from Milan,
> Which gave me some sensations like a villain. (2.209)

"Sensations like a villain" is the right phrase here, for *Don Juan* was written during a particularly virulent period of British government censorship and well-financed private initiatives against "indecent literature." For Byron, the *real* villains were precisely those intolerant laws and social customs – and the outraged mothers and furious fathers who appointed themselves their upholders. Moral standards were as flimsy and arbitrary as ideals of beauty: "But if I *had been* at Timbuctoo, there / No doubt I should be told that black is fair. . . . The whole matter rests upon eye-sight" (12.70–1).

Yet, more profoundly, for Byron Eros itself is the villain: "For soon or late Love is his own avenger" (4.73). Love has unforeseen and often terrible consequences, and not just in lovesickness or venereal disease but because it is doomed to end. Although Byron never finished *Don Juan*, it is clear that its moral was not that those whose love is insatiable will go to hell but, rather, that we had better "hoard up warmth against a wintry day" (10.9). Juan, like all of us, will get old, and his passions will fade. This sad fact applies to even the most ardent of us mortals, and above all, thinks this self-aware poet, to himself.

Indeed, Juan was deliberately meant to be a stand-in for Byron. Born into the British nobility, handsome but suffering from a deformed right foot and lower leg, and almost always in need of money, he studied at Cambridge and then traveled through Europe, ignoring the Napoleonic wars raging around him. From Portugal and Spain, he went to Greece, Albania and Turkey, more or less the path later traced by his Don Juan. Byron swam the Hellespont, took lovers of both sexes, and became famous after publishing the first two cantos of his long poem *Childe Harold's Pilgrimage*. Thereafter he became a sort of matinee idol in this newly consumerist culture (see figure 15), with the difference that his admirers hoped to change his ways. Or, as his future

wife wrote: "Reforming Byron with his magic sway /
Compels all hearts to love him and obey."[26] She too
came under his spell, married him in spite of her doubts,
and soon repented: Byron wrote *Don Juan* in the wake
of their scandalous divorce and in self-imposed exile
from England.

*

Unlike Byron, but much like Sade, Giacomo Casanova
(d. 1798) lived before the reaction to liberal ideas, lib-
ertinism, and political liberty had entrenched itself in
the post-Napoleonic order. An insouciant Don Juan in
the flesh, he was born in Venice, left Italy for Greece,
then went to France. From there he departed for Vienna
and thence back to Venice, where, after a daring escape
from the state prison, he fled to Germany, France, and
the Netherlands. Back to Italy and then, expelled from
various cities there, he went on to London. Onward
further still, to Berlin, then Russia, Poland, eventually
to Spain, and so on. A jet-setter long before jets were
invented. At his last refuge, working as a librarian at
Count Waldstein's castle in Bohemia, he likely helped
da Ponte write a bit of the libretto for *Don Giovanni*.
Everywhere (except in those very final years) he found
beautiful women to love and who loved him in return.
It amused him greatly, he claimed, to write the *Story of
My Life* as he neared old age, for in doing so he recalled
his many past pleasures, adventures, and misadventures.
What he did not say but was clearly also the case: he
was writing an "autofiction," kneading and shaping
his life into a tasty loaf fit for the man of letters that he
always considered himself to be.

Casanova was not an aristocrat like the fictional
Don Juan or the real Sade or Byron. The son of roving
actors, he worked in the eighteenth-century version of a
gig economy, depending on people in high places rather
than on corporations to keep him afloat. His loves were

likewise gigs, depending on need, opportunity, desire, and the promise of pleasure and perhaps of riches. Casanova's one taboo was sex with another man. He slept with a family of sisters, wined and dined at the many hotels he stayed at, had numerous quick fucks, and met a few women he considered marrying. As he reflected on his life, he made mincemeat of Pausanian morality: "If pleasure exists, and we can only enjoy it in life, then life is a happiness. There are misfortunes, of course, as I should be the first to know. But the very existence of these misfortunes proves that the sum of good is greater."[27] Truth to tell, even the misfortunes amused him – at least once he had escaped them.

Many of Casanova's women were as adrift as he – and as opportunistic. Consider the "castrato" Bellino. Casanova first met her at a hotel in Ancona. Her "face seemed to me feminine. And the masculine attire did not prevent my seeing a certain fullness of bosom, which put it into my head that despite the billing, this must be a girl. In this conviction, I made no resistance to the desires which he aroused in me." Bellino was indeed a girl, Teresa. She had studied voice with the great castrato Salimbeni, and when his real castrato protégé died, she took the name of the deceased and lived as if a member of his family in Bologna while waiting to join Salimbeni. But the great teacher died soon thereafter, so that, when she met Casanova, Teresa had nowhere to go. Hence her appeal to him: "Alas my angel! Rescue me from my shame. Take me with you. I do not ask to become your wife, I will only be your loving mistress." The two join forces. Casanova even wants to marry her. But on their way to Bologna to wed, he loses his passport. By the time the two can get together again, Teresa has done a stint as a female singer in Rimini (where women were allowed on stage, as each Italian city had separate rules) and is on her way to perform in Naples for a year. Casanova, meanwhile, has a commission in Constantinople.

The two meet again seventeen years later in Florence, where they have an extremely brief fling – in the time it takes for Teresa's husband to make some hot chocolate! Afterward, she explains to Casanova that she is "still in love" with her husband and stipulates that they henceforth meet only as friends. That very evening she introduces him to her "brother," a young man who is, in fact, her and Casanova's child. Her protector, the duke who arranged for her Neapolitan debut, took care of the boy's upbringing, first with a nurse and later with a music tutor. Now the young man is following his "sister" as she takes on new singing engagements. When Casanova hears news of her a bit later, she is in London and has become "Angela Calori." Some years after that, he meets her in Prague.

Theirs, then, is a life of constant traveling, of snatching pleasure wherever possible, of loving, and of leaving any offspring to the care of others. The deprecated Pausanian life is here the opposite of condemnable. It is lively, satisfying, and fitting, given that people like Casanova and Teresa must always be on the move. As he looks back on his life "in this year 1797, at the age of seventy-two," Casanova admits that "I have delighted in going astray and I have constantly lived in error." He calls his *Life* a "confession," a reference to Rousseau and, before that, to Augustine. Unlike Augustine, however, he offers no self-abnegation in the face of his sinfulness; unlike Rousseau, no airbrushing of his failures. What should he regret or hide?

> My follies are the follies of youth. You will see that I laugh at them, and if you are kind you will laugh at them with me. You will laugh when you discover that I often had no scruples about deceiving nitwits and scoundrels and fools when I found it necessary. As for women, this sort of reciprocal deceit cancels itself out, for when love enters in, both parties are usually dupes.

Casanova believed in God and prayer even as he
regarded himself as a "free agent." He knew his own
nature, rejoiced in his passions, was curious about
everything – even cruelty and corruption – and forgave
his own peccadilloes. He lived for pleasure and was glad
to be alive. Love was his second nature: "I was born for
the sex opposite to mine. I have always loved it and done
all that I could to make myself loved by it." He hoped
that his readers would admire him, "yet I will confess
that I cannot rid myself of the fear of being hissed."

In the ensuing, more censorious century, Casanova
was – if not exactly hissed – bowdlerized. This was the
era of Metternich, the restored French monarchy, the
industrial revolution, and the Victorians. In the United
States, growing concern about "decency" and "corruption of morals" led to court cases such as one in 1815,
when the Commonwealth of Pennsylvania brought suit
against Jesse Sharpless and others for showing a "lewd,
wicked, scandalous, infamous, and obscene painting"
to some young people with intent "to debauch and
corrupt" their morals "and to raise and create in their
minds inordinate and lustful desires."[28] The category
of "pornography" was born in the nineteenth century:
that which is meant to sexually arouse, to "appeal
to the prurient interest," with no other purpose.[29]
Pornography is not insatiable love; its purpose is simply
sexual stimulation.

Lifelong love

At the same time as "decency" became a category with
which to castigate pornography, love was domesticated.
There were plenty of affairs and sex and marriages in
the nineteenth century. But only marriage – or its simulacrum, a love that lasted a lifetime – was celebrated.
"Reader, I married him," begins the short last chapter

166 Love: A History in Five Fantasies

of Charlotte Brontë's *Jane Eyre* (1847). It was meant as the happy culmination of all that went before.

Insatiable love largely disappeared, drowned out by pornography on the one hand and married love on the other. True, in Leo Tolstoy's *Anna Karenina* (1878), Alexei Vronsky is a ladies' man. But that ends when he meets Anna. Thereafter, their love rules their lives, and their story is over when, convinced that Vronsky no longer loves her, Anna hurls herself under a train. Gone is the insouciant Casanova – or, for that matter, Goethe, Byron, and Teresa; they would have shed a tear at losing Vronsky and moved on. Anna could not move on, and Vronsky could not do so either after her suicide. He, too, courted death by volunteering to fight the Turks in Serbia.

Chapters prefaced by quotations from Byron's *Don Juan* in Stendhal's *The Red and the Black* (1830) seem to portend another great womanizer as its protagonist. Hardly! Stendhal's hero, Julien Sorel, has only two love affairs. Born poor, sensitive, ambitious, and a reader, he is an admirer of Napoleon after Waterloo. Julien tries to get ahead. But although he realizes at one level that the "red" of glorious war has given way to the "black" of anti-revolutionary fear, petty hypocrisy, conniving, back-biting, and strategizing, he can never quite manage to adjust to the facts. For, at a more basic level, he despises his society, resents its denigration of men of his class, and wants to rise as a man of pure honor, duty, and glory. He conducts his love affairs (like his other actions) as mini-battles, plotting his moves. Is he ever himself? Not really; he is always playing a role: "He feared that he would be the victim of a fearful disgrace . . . if he departed from the ideal of behavior he had set himself. In a word, what made Julien a superior being was precisely the quality that prevented him from seizing a pleasure that lay directly in his path."[30]

Meanwhile, Julien's second female conquest, Mathilde-Marguerite de La Mole, was playing out a very different fantasy based on the passionate love of Queen Marguerite de Navarre (d. 1549) for an ancestor of de La Mole herself. In the story Mathilde told herself, the love of Queen Marguerite had been so great that, after her lover suffered beheading, she "took that head in her carriage and went to bury it with her own hands."

The only person in the novel who was not play-acting was Julien's first mistress, Mme. de Rênal. Hers was "true love," the fruit of what Stendhal elsewhere calls a "crystallization," when a person realizes that another is so admirable in every way as to be the source of all his or her happiness.[31] That very idea dawns on Mme. de Rênal long before the two have made love. Unfortunately, it takes Julien to the very end of the novel before his love for Mme. de Rênal crystallizes. It's almost too late. In his ultimate heroic gesture, Julien has tried to kill her, giving in to his "Napoleonic" outrage that she had besmirched his honor in a letter. His bullet only grazes her, and they have a passionate reunion in his jail cell. Thereafter he goes cheerfully to his death: "To walk in the open air was for him a delicious experience. . . . There now, things are going very well, he told himself, I shall have no lack of courage." Happy memories of the early days with Mme. de Rênal come flooding back, and, for perhaps the first time in Julien's life, "everything proceeded simply, decently, and without the slightest affectation on his part."[32] In the end, Stendhal upholds Pausanian good love, the steadfast love that lasts a lifetime.

In this he was a man of his age. The outrages of the French aristocracy as painted by Laclos and Sade helped give birth to the ideal, if not the reality, of the companionate marriage (we have already seen in chapter 3 a parallel trajectory in the newly fledged United States). Even after the Restoration of the French monarchy in

1815, popular opinion remained resolutely set against the "dissolute" upper classes, while the ideal of marital bliss was attributed to a "virtuous" middle class. And yet, reflecting the "unrationalized coexistence of sexual mores" in his day, Stendhal himself longed for the life of a Casanova.[33] In his autobiography, after listing (by initials) the twelve women that he had loved in his life, he noted wryly, "In actual fact, I possessed only six of these women." He regretted that "I was not promiscuous, not enough so."[34]

By the second half of the nineteenth century almost everyone in France could read and a new female readership took root. That was the background to Flaubert's *Madame Bovary*, its protagonist so steeped in the romance of Paul and Virginia that she expected reality to mirror it. But not only women had fantasies about love. That was the point of Flaubert's *Sentimental Education* (1869). The ostensible "pupil" receiving the "education" is Frédéric Moreau, who falls in love at first sight with Mme. Arnoux, a married, somewhat older woman: "It was like an apparition: She was sitting in the middle of the bench, all alone; or rather he could not see anybody else in the dazzling light which her eyes cast upon him."[35] Though they almost consummate their love at one point, she is too dutiful a wife and mother to do so. Eventually they drift apart. But the fantasy of their love remains vivid for both. In the end, Frédéric glimpses Mme. Arnoux's gray hair. They are old people; love has passed them by. Their – and the reader's – "sentimental education" is bittersweet, much like the Revolution of 1848 that forms the novel's backdrop. Nursing a fantasy, whether of liberty or of love, is foolhardy. It is easy to do, but best to doubt its importance in the larger scheme of things.

Flaubert was in fact giving himself and his readership an education in sentiment. Even as the fantasy of insatiability was nearly buried, steadfast love was not always the ideal. For Flaubert, love was muse to art. In his mid-teens, Flaubert, like Frédéric, saw a beautiful married woman. The moment shook him to the core: "She looked at me. I lowered my eyes and blushed. What a gaze, indeed! How beautiful this woman was! I can still see that ardent pupil beneath a black brow settling on me like a sun."[36] Thereafter, he claimed, he loved her and only her, though he saw little of her thereafter. She was the dream of love, much as Beatrice had been for Dante and Laura for Petrarch. Flaubert was sensible to love's pleasures; as he wrote to Louise Colet at the beginning of their nearly eight-year-long affair, "I want to cover you with love when I next see you, with caresses, with ecstasy. I want to gorge you with all the joys of the flesh, until you faint and die." But he did not care to be with her very often: in the course of the first two years of their passionate correspondence, he saw her only five times, even though she bitterly complained, and there was no great distance between them. In one sense, Flaubert was as committed to insatiable love as Casanova, but he was committed more to fantasizing about it than to living it. As he explained to Colet, "I enjoy debauchery and I live like a monk." But Louise Colet herself, though married, took on and discarded many lovers, if not with ease, nevertheless with renewed hope each time. As Flaubert wrote to her, "you respect passions and aspire to happiness." Because its literature is so rich, we can see that, for all the nineteenth century's reputation for bourgeois respectability and its emphasis on decency, the life of the libertine lured many.

Eros unbound

Towards the end of the nineteenth century, Richard von Krafft-Ebing (d. 1902) and, shortly thereafter, Sigmund Freud (d. 1939) put sex and love under the microscope.

As we saw in chapter 2, physicians had for centuries offered various cures for obsessive love. But their rudimentary notions of lovesickness were much too simple for nineteenth-century scientists. Krafft-Ebing's *Psychopathia sexualis* (1886) did for sex what Linnaeus had done for species: he gave names to each pathological (and, by implication, "normal") form. Along with a few other medical writers, he popularized the terms "homosexual" and "heterosexual" as well as varieties of sexual "deviation," such as masochism, sadism, and fetishism. He declared that a "sex drive" was at the bottom of all this diversity.

In using the term "drive," Krafft-Ebing was drawing on a strain of German thought dating from a century before in the writings of Herder and Schiller. It postulated that there were two drives: one (hunger) for self-preservation, the other (sex) for reproduction. Such ideas were implicit in Goethe's Faust, the striver and womanizer *par excellence*. What exactly the drives were, whether they were innate or a product of experience, where precisely they were located physically (if anywhere) – all were up for debate. When Krafft-Ebing entered the fray, it was to assert that the drives were universally human. In its raw form the drive for reproduction was the same as "unbridled love," which he described as "a volcano that burns down and lays waste all around it; it is an abyss that devours all – honor, substance, and health."[37] Love's "bridles" (the idea surely came from Plato) were, he said, morality, upbringing, education, and heredity, all of which bound it to its proper purpose – reproduction – or, in unfortunate instances, thrust it into deviant paths. Krafft-Ebing's book was filled with mini-case histories detailing the early experiences that triggered adult abnormalities. His links were direct and simple: for example, he explained that a young woman wanted to be spanked by the men she loved because, as a girl, she had been jokingly spanked by the father of her girlfriend.

But Krafft-Ebing also attributed wider and more profound effects to the sex drive: "Few people are conscious of the deep influence exerted by sexual life upon the sentiment, thought, and action of man in his social relations to others." This idea became increasingly important to Freud as he worked towards a unified theory that would account for both normal and pathological mental life. If the sex drive was behind "thought and action," it was equally the propellant of "artistic achievements, religious and altruistic feelings, etc."[38] Freud, too, arrived at the sex drive, but he rightly claimed to have "extended the concept of what is sexual far beyond its usual range."[39]

Freud came to speak of "infantile sexuality": not just the sexuality that begins at puberty but the sexuality of children at their mother's breast. Babies find pleasure not only in satisfying their hunger but also in the sensations of sucking. Soon they discover erogenous zones beyond their mouth, indeed over all the surfaces of their body. From the start, their sexual drive is inextricably tied to love. At first it is the love that they feel for their mother and soon for both their parents; later it is bound to other objects and pursuits.

For Freud, the experiences and (above all) the fantasies of childhood shape adult development in every way, not just sexual behavior. True, the goal of the sex drive is to revel in sensuous pleasure, but those very pleasures come with mental representations in the forms of ideas, fantasies, and idealizations. In sublimated form, and by circuitous routes, the sex drive is also the seed from which blossoms art, music, and knowledge of every sort. Like Krafft-Ebing, Freud filled his works with case histories, but Freud's were far longer because, for him, mental health did not depend on a few interviews to determine past precedents. Rather, the experiences that really mattered in adult life, he said, had long been "repressed" from consciousness. They could be uncovered and brought to light only with long therapy. No one who suffers from mental illness gets better by knowing that, for example, a friend's father once pretended to spank her. She gets better by going through the painful experience of unearthing materials long buried with the help of a therapist to whom she has "formed a sufficient attachment (transference) . . . to make a fresh flight impossible." This "transference love" is the key to the psychoanalytic experience and to a healthy outcome. Patients fall in love with their therapists. Their therapists, half in love themselves, must consider the feelings as "something unreal," avatars of unconscious fantasies which, once attended to, may be controlled.[40] In short, adult love repeats the patterns of infantile love, and transference love does so even more directly than most. Once the repetition is brought to light, so too are all the unacceptable, frightening, and repugnant feelings, thoughts, and fantasies once thrust by the superego into the abyss of the unconscious.

For Freud, Eros permeates the whole of life, whether awake, asleep, or engaged in creative pursuits and occupations that matter to us. The goal of therapy is to release repressed elements of the sex drive, not so that our sexual impulses may have free reign, which would itself be pathological, but to allow us to enjoy more fully the pleasures available to us. Either one of Pausanias' loves would do, and so would others Pausanias never thought of. For it is perfectly Freudian to argue that people's emotions are normally ambivalent: we love, hate, fear, and desire the same people and things – all at the same time. This is the dynamic of the so-called Oedipus complex: "The hate which resulted from the rivalry for the mother could not permeate the boy's psychic life without being inhibited; he had to contend with the tenderness and admiration which he had felt for his father from the beginning."[41]

*

We might imagine that the post-Freudian world would celebrate or at least look kindly upon all sorts of loves and sexualities, since the avowed purpose of psychoanalysis was to enhance the patient's "capacity for love."[42] And that is certainly partially true. Today many accept gay marriages, transgender marriages, open marriages. Laura Kipnis argues with perky insouciance that life-long love is a mirage: "domestic coupledom" is "modern love's mandatory barracks."[43] Pascal Bruckner suggests dissociation: live together, yet, if you like, love and desire elsewhere.[44] Some people choose polyamory, having romantic and sexual (or intimate albeit asexual) relationships with the consent of all. By contrast, others (mainly women, it seems) opt for "self-marriages" involving tradition-inspired weddings: invitations to family and friends, a walk down the aisle, a ring, flowers, cake, and wedding vows, such as (in one YouTube video): "To take excellent care of myself, practically, financially and physically; to support my creative practice; to nourish my adventurous spirit; to take more risks in matters of the heart; and to commit to my own personal journey in personal transformation so that I could help everybody else do the same."[45] In response to this particular video, one commenter dryly wrote: "So how was the wedding night?" Fanny Hill could have answered this decisively centuries ago.

Yet it remains true that, even today, many put a premium on life-long love. The critique of modern love by Jean-Claude Kaufmann, mentioned in chapter 3, offers the hope that the historical conflict between empathy and passion will come to an end with couples learning to extend unconditional love to their partner.

In Larry Kramer's *Faggots*, a bitter satire of gay life before the AIDS epidemic, the hero, Fred Lemish, at first seems to want the life of a homosexual Casanova. But Casanova had been able to remember all his partners and got pleasure from every episode, whereas when Fred begins to chronicle his numerous sexual encounters he is "dismayed at how many of the names he no longer remembered. Who were Bat, Ivan, Tommy, Sam Jellu . . ., too many of the 23, not to mention the 87, were now unrecognizable and obviously equally as unmemorable as the how many – ? 100? 200? 50? 23? orgasms he had probably forgotten to tally."[46] Despite his life of cruising, sexual adventures to rival Nanna's, and casual fucks in every venue, Fred longs for true love, a house in the country, a "happily ever after." Is Dinky "the One"? Fred goes through contortions to sort out what he really wants. "No, [life-long love] doesn't have to be a fantasy. I'm beginning to think that the only fantasy is Dinky. He's beginning to look less and less like a housewife. Or a husband." He moves on, finds yet another "lean and youthful gorgeousness," and he's "falling again, falling into fantasy again, . . . turning a Hot Number into love."

Fantasies of love mingle and jostle together, and all entice. Fred longs for the mutual obligations and harmonious like-mindedness of an ideal marriage. At the same time, he needs to be obsessed with Dinky (or another "youthful gorgeousness"), so beautiful, so desirable, and so distant as to give his life meaning. Beyond all that is the lure of the "next," the insatiable restlessness that drives Eros on to "The Titillating! The Turn-On! The Permutations of yet another ringing change on sex." Luckily, somehow, at the very end, Fred's "eyes turn toward land." Has he escaped the pull of fantasies? I would say that he has simply found yet another one, akin to marrying himself: "I want to change. I must change myself. Be my own Mom and

Pop. Be strong enough for Me." That too is a fantasy, one of total self-sufficiency.

Insatiable love is the heart of darkness, the threat of unchained desire. It is precisely its lowliness that gives it the sheen of rebellious daring, striking sparks off "decent" loves. And perhaps that is its purpose, its *raison d'être* – the fantasy that disrupts and tempts the others: the Dionysian frenzy of the ancient world, the lust of medieval vices, the ravening id of the Freudians in the early twentieth century. And in our own time? Today, as always, it is a way to experiment, redefine decency, and play with norms. Pausanias was outraged by men who loved women; Peter Damien, a medieval churchman, was scandalized by men who loved men; in the twentieth century Fred Lemish is dismayed by his own insatiability. It's hard to predict the next frontier to be breached, but surely Resourcefulness and Need will find it.

Conclusion

When Stendhal's Mathilde de La Mole told Julien Sorel that he should climb a ladder to her bedroom, unlike Diotima, she didn't mean for him to ascend to virtue. She wanted him to be her lover, one such as Queen Marguerite had had in the sixteenth century. Or so she imagined. But once Julien arrived in her room, she felt nothing but obligation. She thought that she ought to follow through with her part, and so she did. But afterward, she was disappointed: she felt only "misery and shame . . . instead of those divine raptures that novels talked about." For his part, Julien was equally put off. He had been "pursuing the phantom of a mistress who should be naturally tender and give not a thought to her own existence as soon as she had made her lover happy."[1] Mathilde was not that mistress. And yet the two continued to see each other, to imagine that they were in love, and to plan for a life together.

Fantasies help organize and give shape to feelings that are otherwise inchoate. It's not that love doesn't exist; it does exist, but "it" is not one thing. Affection, tenderness, desire, anger, hatred, resentment, need, duty, honor, hurt, scorn, grief, despair, shame, ambition, and calculation all may mingle together to form it. Only indifference is the precise opposite of love. Because it is so complex, we try to tame it with categories: the short, crisp word "Love" is itself such a category. All the commonplace sayings about love with which this book began constitute further attempts to pin it down and even give it moral significance.

Love stories provide potent crystallizations: they give love scripts and models to follow and reveal its rewards. Freud called transference love "something unreal." But even he knew that this was not the whole truth. *All* loves are like transference love, based as they are on our feelings, life experiences, and modes of understanding these things – including our fantasies. Whether we like it or not, illusions (from children's play-acting to QAnon) are very much part of reality; make-believe is our way to make sense – and to make art – out of a congeries of disparate elements.

Fantasies of love are potent. Indeed, they may be wielded as instruments of power. It is easy to see this in the case of Mathilde with her melodramatic fixation on her ancestor's story: she made her idea of the love of Queen Marguerite her own – and she made Julien's fate that of Marguerite's lover. After he was executed, Mathilde took possession of his severed head and buried it – playing to the hilt her fantasy of the sixteenth-century queen.

The script that Mathilde followed was hers alone. It never gained assent as a "universal truth" about love. But many love stories with long histories have continued to influence generations over the long haul. The idea that love means finding "another self" is as old as Homer. So too is the fantasy that love is an obsession, so memorably symbolized by Penelope's constant weeping and the troubadours' endless longing. The idea that love takes us out of this world has its antecedents in Diotima's speech in Plato's *Symposium* and the religious mysticism of the Middle Ages. Pausanias reveals that the notion of insatiable love was well known in his day. But while it was accepted as the erotic behavior of the gods, it became an ideal for *human* love only when it was wielded against the strictures of Church and State and when the printing press made its general diffusion possible. By contrast with these narratives, the widespread fantasy that modern love is obligation-free derives from a misreading of history and a mistaken view of past oppression.

Slowly, through these disparate fantasies, the richly varied outlines of a history of love emerge. Although most of the stories they tell are dominated by men, women have not been passive listeners to male fantasies but, rather, have embroidered, appropriated, and refashioned them for their own purposes. Saint Perpetua reworked the transcendent ascent envisaged by Plato into the arduous climb of the martyr a generation before Origen reformulated the idea for Christian celibates. When Heloise declared that she would rather be Abelard's mistress than his wife, she was repudiating centuries of ecclesiastical teaching as she declared that love should be freely given and taken, not bound by vows. Jeanne de Montbaston, who depicted a nun gathering penises from a tree (figure 10), skewered the Church long before Aretino had Nanna making love to a rich assortment of monks and priests. *Trobairitz*, the women troubadours, loved as longingly and bitterly as any male troubadour. Marie de Gournay, Montaigne's eager editor, did what she could to give the lie to the idea that only men could be friends in the "other self" tradition.

Yet, on the whole, male voices predominate in Western fantasies of love, even when they purport to take the part of women. Men dominate the narratives of love's duties, rewards, pains, and moral value. They are the ones to offer models of love that are, whether explicitly or implicitly, meant to shape who loves whom, for how long, and for what reasons. Augustine of Hippo made human love dependent on the Christian God.

The Church – dominated by men at every level – institutionalized scriptural teachings by writing them into marriage vows. Plato animated the voice of Diotima to offer a vision of love's transcendent purpose, while Casanova proclaimed love's pleasures to be its essence. Even so, it may be that men's voices seem stronger than women's only because the female contributions to history, music, art, and philosophy have been played down. Some of the poems in Goethe's romantic poem cycle *Suleika* were in fact written by his mistress, Marianne von Willemer. At least one of Abelard's most original philosophical ideas appears to have been suggested first by Heloise. And perhaps there really had been a Diotima!

*

The ancient Greeks fostered multiple gods and tolerated numerous fantasies of love. Trotted out and, no doubt, tried on (much as young men wore the outfit sported by Werther as they played the part of the hopeless lover), these stories came into particular favor at various times as they were practiced by different emotional communities. Or they came together to be probed and debated, as happened in the lively discussions of Plato's *Symposium*. But the wild variety of ancient erotic models was eventually tamed by the Roman juggernaut and proclaimed to be at an end by Augustus, who backed up his restrictions with legislation. Even so, the old fantasies persisted "underground." That was true even during the most serious attempts to stamp them out and impose one standard fantasy of love – the one implicit in the letters of Paul and pseudo-Paul and gradually enshrined in canon law. Even as that single love story became institutionalized in the eleventh and twelfth centuries, as the Church began to take over marital practices previously controlled by private families, the flames of the old fantasies persisted. They were fanned in schoolrooms, elaborated at the courts of the wealthy, and welcomed in bawdy fabliaux for and by common folk. Then, too, it would be wrong to think that only one fantasy dominated in all Church venues: the ecstatic love of the Song of Songs permeated the monasteries, where the passion for God trod much the same path as the troubadour's longing for his lady. Nor has this book been able to consider the numerous fantasies of love – some as "Western" as those traced here – that were undoubtedly cultivated in Muslim, Jewish, and so-called heretical communities. Meanwhile, as we have seen, the mainstream fantasies proliferated, branched out, and took new forms.

With the printing press, the fragmentation of religious confessions during the Reformation, the rise of nation-states, and the resultant space for people to critique both ecclesiastical and political institutions, fantasies of love so luxuriant in the ancient world now mingled with Christian ideals or flourished in determined opposition to them. Thus, at about the same time as the irreverent Pietro Aretino made unbridled sex the only form of love, Michel de Montaigne celebrated his bond with the like-minded La Boétie, Protestant circles found transcendence through love of children, and many people continued to take traditional marriage vows, whether in Catholic or Protestant lands. Passions were high, and debates about love were equally battles about God. Thus, the very factors that allowed so many ideas about love to flourish at the same time also fostered the outbreak of a century and more of religious wars.

War and love? The two were never so separate as the chant "Make love, not war" of the 1960s suggested. Certainly, the links between power, love, and sex have always been clear. Plato and Aristotle explored them in their writings on both ethics and politics. Obedience, which by definition implies a hierarchy of power, was enshrined in Christian culture: in monasteries, where the monks were "brothers" while the abbot was the "father" and God loomed over all; in feudal relations; in traditional marriage vows; and in the service love poets sang about. So ingrained was the association between hegemony and sex that, when Europeans conquered the Americas, they thought of "her" as a willing voluptuary. The characters in *Dangerous Liaisons* brandished love as a weapon with which to manipulate others. On the other hand, when advertisers claim "You'll just love our cereal," the word nearly loses its force.

Nearly, but not entirely. For, even while ardent words may always be routinized and misappropriated, they may also be sincere. Or manipulative and sincere at the same time. Sometimes the lover himself doesn't quite know which he is pursuing; as Valmont learned, love can turn around and bite you even when you think you have your armor on.

Today we are heir to the whole panoply of Western stories and more as well: love traditions from Africa, Asia, South Asia, and indigenous American groups. Yet it is easy for people to adhere to one fantasy and let it dominate their lives. Heloise was locked into a story of love freely given and taken between lovers whose thoughts mirrored one another; early in life Dante found in Beatrice a source of transcendence that he would never relinquish. Marjorie Hansen Shaevitz's husband insisted, in the face of his wife's busy career, that wives had the obligation to take care of their men. Bess Gornick, widowed early, remained obsessed with the memory of her husband for the rest of her life. Goethe imagined that Faust was redeemed by his love – and abandonment – of Margareta because it was in the nature of men to strive after "eternal womanhood."

But Casanova, who did indeed pursue women endlessly, was willing to toss aside that narrative of love in order to marry Teresa. Their marriage might not have ended up as the life-long love of Christian vows, but at least Casanova was open to it. Over the long haul, fantasies of love have been turned around, reconceived, and repurposed. This is a liberating idea. History has two primary uses: to see what things were like in the past and to see how they changed over time. It provides distance and perspective. The history of love as a tangle of disparate fantasies is no different. The models, ideals, hopes, and imaginings that have undergirded love are there to be understood, their transformations appreciated, their manifestations critiqued. "What is love?" asks philosopher Simon May at the beginning of one book. I ask, instead: "What has love been?" The fantasies people have today seem to have been around forever; they appear to be built in and "natural." Their histories prove that to be the most misleading fantasy of all. When Jackie Wilson sang "your love keeps lifting me," he was sounding yet one more variation on an idea that had once been a philosopher's attempt to transcend change and mortality, a medieval Christian's desire to ascend to God, a poet's salvation through the image of a girl on the streets of Florence. It's a beautiful idea, but if it sets up expectations that are not – and never will be – met, it can be jettisoned. We may, if our disappointment is intense, consider therapies such as that advocated by Angus and Greenberg, which strive to change the narrative we cling to as individuals, born of our personal experiences.[2] In my view, knowing love's history may also be – is – a kind of therapy, helping free us from stories that appear to be fixed and true for all time. If they don't work for us, we may find – or create – new ones.

I became a historian in part to rebel against the limits of Freud's theories, which made so much of the interplay of universals (such as the Oedipal complex) and individual neuroses (as repressed childhood fantasies) but nothing of the temper of an age or our dependence on circumstance and contingency. Yet, as I learned while researching and writing this book, history itself offers up fantasies. They change with the times, as does their relevance and the experiences they compass; and yet, despite all that, they continue to glow and beckon. Knowing their contexts and their vagaries helps us put them in perspective and free us from their tyranny.

Notes

Introduction

1 Barbara H. Rosenwein, ed., *Anger's Past: The Social Uses of an Emotion in the Middle Ages* (Ithaca, NY, 1998).
2 Joanna Bourke, *Fear: A Cultural History* (Emeryville, CA, 2005); Darrin M. McMahon, *Happiness: A History* (New York, 2006); Barbara H. Rosenwein, *Emotional Communities in the Early Middle Ages* (Ithaca, NY, 2006).
3 Barbara H. Rosenwein, *Generations of Feeling: A History of Emotions, 600–1700* (Cambridge, 2016).
4 Barbara H. Rosenwein, *Anger: The Conflicted History of an Emotion* (London, 2020).
5 Arlie Russell Hochschild, *Strangers in Their Own Land: Anger and Mourning on the American Right* (New York, 2016), pp. 6, 135.
6 L. E. Angus and L. S. Greenberg, *Working with Narrative in Emotion-Focused Therapy: Changing Stories, Healing Lives* (Washington, DC, 2011); Iiro P. Jääskeläinen, Vasily Klucharev, Ksenia Panidi, and Anna N. Shestakova, "Neural Processing of Narratives: From Individual Processing to Viral Propagation," *Frontiers in Human Neuroscience*

14 (2020), doi: 10.3389/fnhum.2020.00253; Joan Didion, "The White Album," in *We Tell Ourselves Stories in Order to Live: Collected Nonfiction* (New York, 2006), p. 185.

7 Maddie Dai, cartoon, *The New Yorker* (December 16, 2019), p. 37.

8 Simon May, *Love: A History* (New Haven, CT, 2011), p. 2.

Chapter 1 Like-Mindedness

1 *Enlightened*, season 1, episode 6, at bit.ly/3kxjA 4x.

2 Homer, *The Odyssey*, trans. Peter Green (Oakland, CA, 2018); all quotations cited by book and line number.

3 Ellen D. Reeder, *Pandora: Women in Classical Greece* (Princeton, NJ, 1995), p. 23.

4 Plato, *Laws* 8.836a–837d, trans. Trevor J. Saunders, in *Plato: Complete Works*, ed. John M. Cooper (Indianapolis, 1997), pp. 1498–9.

5 Plato, *Symposium*, trans. Alexander Nehamas and Paul Woodruff (Indianapolis, 1989), cited by section number.

6 Aristotle, *Nicomachean Ethics*, trans. Terence Irwin (2nd edn, Indianapolis, 1999), cited by section number.

7 Cicero, *Laelius on Friendship*, in Cicero, *De senectute, de amicitia, de divinatione*, trans. William Armistead Falconer (Cambridge, 1923), cited by chapter and section number.

8 Craig A. Williams, *Roman Homosexuality* (2nd edn, Oxford, 2010).

9 Cicero, *Letters to Atticus*, ed. and trans. D. R. Shackleton Bailey, vol 1: *68–59 BC* (Cambridge, 1965), no. 18, pp. 171–3.

10 Augustine, *The Confessions of St. Augustine*, trans. Rex Warner (New York, 1963), cited by book and section number.
11 Augustine, *On the Trinity, Books 8–15*, ed. Gareth B. Matthews, trans. Stephen McKenna (Cambridge, 2002), cited by book and section number.
12 Augustine, Letter 93 in *Letters*, Vol. 2 (83–130), trans. Wilfrid Parsons (Washington, DC, 1953), p. 60.
13 Hildesheim letter collection, Letter 36 (c. 1073–85), quoted in C. Stephen Jaeger, *Ennobling Love: In Search of a Lost Sensibility* (Philadelphia, 1999), pp. 218–19.
14 Goscelin of St Bertin, *The Book of Encouragement and Consolation [Liber confortatorius]*, trans. Monika Otter (Cambridge, 2004), pp. 19, 21.
15 Aelred of Rievaulx, *Spiritual Friendship*, trans. Lawrence C. Braceland (Collegeville, MN, 2010), cited by book and section number.
16 For the first collection: Abelard and Heloise, *The Letters and Other Writings*, trans. William Levitan (Indianapolis, 2007), cited as Levitan with page number; for the second collection, anonymous but quite certainly by Abelard and Heloise: *Making Love in the Twelfth Century: "Letters of Two Lovers" in Context*, ed. and trans. Barbara Newman (Philadelphia, 2016), cited as Newman with page number.
17 Michel de Montaigne, "Friendship," in *Selected Essays with La Boétie's Discourse on Voluntary Servitude*, trans. James B. Atkinson and David Sices (Indianapolis, 2012), pp. 74, 80, 81.
18 Michel de Montaigne, "Of Diversion," Essay 3.4 in *The Complete Works*, trans. Donald M. Frame (New York, 2003), p. 769.
19 Montaigne, "Friendship," p. 74.
20 David Lewis Schaefer, ed. *Freedom over Servitude:*

Montaigne, La Boétie, and On Voluntary Servitude (Westport, CT, 1998).
21 Étienne de La Boétie, *Poemata*, ed. James S. Hirstein, trans. Robert D. Cottrell, *Montaigne Studies* no. 3 (1991): 15–47, at p. 27.
22 La Boétie, *Discourse on Voluntary Servitude*, in Montaigne, *Selected Essays*, pp. 286, 289.
23 Appendix II: The Twenty-Nine Sonnets, trans. Randolph Paul Runyon, in *Freedom over Servitude*, pp. 224–35.
24 Montaigne, "Friendship," p. 77.
25 Montaigne, "Being Presumptuous," in *Selected Essays*, p. 175.
26 Montaigne, *Les essais* [1595 edn], ed. Denis Bjaï, Bénédicte Boudou, Jean Céard, and Isabelle Pantin (Paris, 2001), pp. 25, 31, 43, 48.
27 Montaigne, "Friendship," p. 79.
28 David Hume, *A Treatise of Human Nature*, ed. David Fate Norton and Mary J. Norton (Oxford, 2001), cited by book, chapter, section, and paragraph number.
29 Marco Iacoboni, "The Human Mirror System and its Role in Imitation and Empathy," in *The Primate Mind: Built to Connect with Other Minds*, ed. Pier Francesco Ferrari et al. (Cambridge, 2012), p. 42.
30 Jan Rostowski, "Selected Aspects of the Neuropsychology of Love," *Acta Neuropsychologica* 7/4 (2009): 240.
31 Alan Bray, *The Friend* (Chicago, 2003), p. 1.
32 Quoted in E. Anthony Rotundo, "Romantic Friendship: Male Intimacy and Middle-Class Youth in the Northern United States, 1800–1900," *Journal of Social History* 23/1 (1989): 1–25.
33 Laura Gowing, Michael Hunter, and Miri Rubin, eds, *Love, Friendship and Faith in Europe, 1300–1800* (Basingstoke, 2005), p. 3.

34 Annie Proulx, *Brokeback Mountain* (New York, 1997), pp. 12, 15, 53.
35 Rotundo, "Romantic Friendship," p. 15.
36 Carroll Smith-Rosenberg, "The Female World of Love and Ritual: Relations between Women in Nineteenth-Century America," *Signs* 1/1 (1975): 1–29, at p. 4.
37 Elena Ferrante, *My Brilliant Friend*, trans. Ann Goldstein (New York, 2012), pp. 1, 18.
38 David Zucchino and Fatima Faizi, "After Losing His Legs to a Bomb, Afghan Veteran Is on a New Journey," *New York Times* (January 26, 2020), at nyti.ms/30kgbsv.
39 Kate Rose, *You Only Fall in Love Three Times: The Secret Search for Our Twin Flame* (New York, 2020), p. 140.

Chapter 2 Transcendence

1 Jackie Wilson, "(Your Love Keeps Lifting Me) Higher and ...". Lyrics by Raynard Miner, Billy Davis, and Gary Jackson, 1967 © Sony/ATV Music Publishing LLC, Warner Chappell Music, Inc., at bit.ly/31dL1c3. Youtube video at bit.ly/36wVNdq. For background, see Wikipedia entry at bit.ly/31PYJ4S.
2 Bella Chagall, *First Encounter*, trans. Barbara Bray (New York, 1983), p. 228.
3 Plato, *Symposium*, trans. Alexander Nehamas and Paul Woodruff (Indianapolis, 1989), cited by section number.
4 Lucretius, *De rerum natura*, 3.894–6, in *Lucretius: On the Nature of Things*, trans. Martin Ferguson Smith (Indianapolis, 2001), p. 91.
5 Thomas J. Heffernan, ed. and trans., *The Passion of Perpetua and Felicity* (Oxford, 2012), pp. 127, 128, 130, 133.

6 Origen, *The Song of Songs: Commentary and Homilies*, trans. R. P. Lawson (Westminster, MD, 1957), pp. 24, 270.

7 Bruce L. Venarde, ed. and trans., *The Rule of Saint Benedict* (Cambridge, 2011), cited by chapter and line number.

8 Bernard of Clairvaux, *On the Song of Songs*, trans. Kilian Walsh, vols. 1 and 2 (Kalamazoo, MI, 1971, 1976), cited by vol. and page number. Biblical quotes here are from this translation.

9 Marguerite Porete, *The Mirror of Simple Souls*, trans. Ellen L. Babinsky (New York, 1993), pp. 198–9, 162, 181, 141, 134, 189, 190–1, 135, 109.

10 Dante Alighieri, *Vita Nuova*, trans. Dino S. Cervigni and Edward Vasta (Notre Dame, IN, 1995), pp. 47, 49, 51, 111.

11 Dante Alighieri, *The Divine Comedy*, trans. Charles S. Singleton, 3 vols (Princeton, 1970–5), Inferno II.72.

12 Purgatorio XXX.46–8; 128–9.

13 Paradiso I.68–9.

14 Ibid., XXXIII.80–1.

15 Quoted in *Luther on Women: A Sourcebook*, ed. and trans. Susan Karant-Nunn and Merry Wiesner-Hanks (Cambridge, 2003), p. 200.

16 Richard Baxter, *A Christian Directory*, vol. 3 (London, 1825), pp. 106–7.

17 Isaac Ambrose, *The Well-Ordered Family* (Boston, 1762), p. 13.

18 "Part of an Address, Written for One of the Maternal Associations of Newark," *Mother's Magazine* 7 (1839): 173–6, at 174; bit.ly/37gxdBJ.

19 Ann Taylor, "My Mother," in Doris Mary Armitage, *The Taylors of Ongar* (Cambridge, 1939), pp. 181–2; bit.ly/36ySdTR.

20 Mary Elliott [Belson], *My Father: A Poem Illustrated with Engravings* (Philadelphia, 1817).

21 *Autobiography of Thomas Wright, of Birkenshaw, in the County of York, 1736–1797*, ed. Thomas Wright (London, 1864), p. 313.
22 [Hannah] Robertson, *The Life of Mrs. Robertson . . . A Tale of Truth as Well as of Sorrow* (Edinburgh, 1792), pp. v, 26.
23 Simon May, *Love: A New Understanding of an Ancient Emotion* (Oxford, 2019), p. xvii.
24 Harry G. Frankfurt, *The Reasons of Love* (Princeton, NJ, 2006), pp. 42, 30, 87.
25 Stephen Sondheim and Leonard Bernstein, "Somewhere," lyrics © 1956, 1957, Amberson Holdings LLC and Stephen Sondheim, at www.westsidestory.com/somewhere.
26 Chagall, *First Encounter*, p. 228.

Chapter 3 Obligation

1 Erich Segal, *Love Story* (New York, 1970), pp. 131, 73.
2 Paul McCartney and John Lennon, "All You Need Is Love," lyrics © Sony/atv Tunes LLC (1967), at bit.ly/2QJE25N.
3 *Missale ad usum . . . Sarum*, ed. Francis H. Dickinson (Burntisland, 1861–83), 831–2*.
4 Zygmunt Bauman, *Liquid Love: On the Frailty of Human Bonds* (Cambridge, 2003).
5 Jean-Claude Kaufmann, *The Curious History of Love*, trans. David Macey (Cambridge, 2011).
6 Stephanie Coontz, *Marriage, a History: How Love Conquered Marriage* (New York, 2005).
7 Homer, *The Odyssey*, trans. Peter Green (Oakland, CA, 2018), cited by book and line number.
8 Hesiod, *Works and Days*, lines 1012–18, in *Theogony* and *Works and Days*, trans. Catherine

M. Schlegel and Henry Weinfield (Ann Arbor, 2006), p. 4.

9 Plato, *Laws* 4.721a, trans. Trevor J. Saunders, in *Plato: Complete Works*, ed. John M. Cooper (Indianapolis, 1997), p. 1407.

10 Thucydides, *History of the Peloponnesian War* 2.44, trans. Rex Warner (London, 1972), p. 150.

11 Xenophon, *Oeconomicus*, trans. Carnes Lord, in *The Shorter Socratic Writings*, ed. Robert C. Bartlett (Ithaca, NY, 1996), cited by chapter and section.

12 Kathleen Freeman, *The Murder of Herodes and Other Trials from the Athenian Law Courts* (Indianapolis, 1994), p. 44.

13 Musonius Rufus, "What is the Chief End of Marriage?," in *Musonius Rufus: "The Roman Socrates,"* ed. and trans. Cora E. Lutz (New Haven, CT, 1947), p. 89.

14 Plutarch, *Advice to the Bride and Groom* 34.142, in *Plutarch's Advice to the Bride and Groom* and *A Consolation to His Wife*, ed. and trans. Sarah B. Pomeroy (New York, 1999), p. 10.

15 Cicero, *Selected Letters*, trans. P. G. Walsh (Oxford, 2008), p. 61.

16 Quoted in Susan Treggiari, *Roman Marriage: Iusti Coniuges from the Time of Cicero to the Time of Ulpian* (Oxford, 1991), p. 212.

17 Ibid., pp. 232–3.

18 Susan Treggiari, "Women in Roman Society," in Diana E. E. Kleiner and Susan B. Matheson, eds, *I Claudia: Women in Ancient Rome* (New Haven, CT, 1996), p. 121.

19 Anne Duncan, "The Roman *Mimae*: Female Performers in Ancient Rome," in Jan Sewell and Clare Smout, eds, *The Palgrave Handbook of the History of Women on Stage* (Cham, 2020), p. 39.

20 Hugh of Saint Victor, *On the Sacraments of the*

Christian Faith (*De sacramentis*) 2.11.3, trans. Roy J. Deferrari (Cambridge, 1951), pp. 325–6.

21 Aelred of Rievaulx, *A Rule of Life for a Recluse*, in *Treatises* and *The Pastoral Prayer*, trans. Mary Paul Macpherson (Spencer, MA, 1971), pp. 80–1.

22 Rosemary Drage Hale, "Joseph as Mother: Adaptation and Appropriation in the Construction of Male Virtue," in *Medieval Mothering*, ed. John Carmi Parsons and Bonnie Wheeler (New York, 1996), p. 105.

23 Dhuoda, *Handbook for William: A Carolingian Woman's Counsel for her Son*, trans. Carol Neel (Washington, DC, 1991), p. 2.

24 Roberd of Brunnè [Robert Mannyng], *Handlyng Synne, with the French Treatise on Which it is Founded, Le Manuel des Pechiez*, ed. Frederick J. Furnivall (London, 1862), p. 345.

25 *Paston Letters and Papers of the Fifteenth Century*, pt I, ed. Norman David (Oxford, 2004), p. 342.

26 *The Good Wife's Guide: Le Ménagier de Paris, a Medieval Household Book*, trans. Gina L. Greco and Christine M. Rose (Ithaca, NY, 2009), pp. 50, 108, 110.

27 Christine de Pizan, *The Book of the City of Ladies*, trans. Earl Jeffrey Richards (rev. edn, New York, 1998), pp. 11, 255.

28 Quoted in Fabrizio Titone, "The Right to Consent and Disciplined Dissent: Betrothals and Marriages in the Diocese of Catania in the Later Medieval Period," in Fabrizio Titone, ed., *Disciplined Dissent: Strategies of Non-Confrontational Protest in Europe from the Twelfth to the Early Sixteenth Century* (Rome, 2016), p. 150, n. 40.

29 Anonymous, *The Art of Courtship; or The School of Love* (London, ?1750), pp. 1–5.

30 Quoted in Nicole Eustace, *Passion Is the Gale: Emotion, Power, and the Coming of the*

American Revolution (Chapel Hill, NC, 2008), p. 120.

31 John Donne, "To His Mistress Going to Bed" [1654], Poetry Foundation, bit.ly/3396BAm.

32 Charlotte Brontë, *Jane Eyre* (New York, 1899), p. 550.

33 Gustave Flaubert, *Madame Bovary*, trans. Lowell Bair (New York, 1972), pp. 31–5, 140, 147.

34 See Karen Lystra, *Searching the Heart: Women, Men, and Romantic Love in Nineteenth-Century America* (New York, 1989), from which all the letters in this section are taken, pp. 32, 14, 36, 197.

35 Marie Carmichael Stopes, *Married Love: A New Contribution to the Solution of Sex Difficulties* (London, 1919), pp. 93, 108.

36 Elinor Glyn, *The Philosophy of Love* (Auburn, NY, 1923), pp. 220–1, 226, 216.

37 U.S. Department of Labor, Women's Bureau, at bit.ly/3nem7m6.

38 Arlie Russell Hochschild with Anne Machung, *The Second Shift: Working Families and the Revolution at Home* (new edn, New York, 2012), p. 4. Similar statistics hold for Eastern and Western European countries: see Lina Gálvez-Muñoz, Paula Rodríguez-Modroño, and Mónica Domínguez-Serrano, "Work and Time Use by Gender: A New Clustering of European Welfare Systems," *Feminist Economics* 17/4 (2011): 125–57, at p. 137.

39 Lawrence A. Kurdek, "The Allocation of Household Labor by Partners in Gay and Lesbian Couples," *Journal of Family Issues* 28 (2007): 132–48.

40 Hochschild and Machung, *The Second Shift*, p. 7.

41 Arlie Russell Hochschild, *The Managed Heart: Commercialization of Human Feeling* (Berkeley, CA, 1983).

42 Gemma Hartley, *Fed Up: Emotional Labor, Women, and the Way Forward* (New York, 2018), p. 7.

43 Hochschild, *The Managed Heart*, p. 194.
44 Jamie K. McCallum, *Worked Over: How Round-the-Clock Work is Killing the American Dream* (New York, 2020), pp. 136, 147.
45 Quoted in Hochschild, *Second Shift*, pp. 27–8.
46 Anthony Giddens, *The Transformation of Intimacy: Sexuality, Love and Eroticism in Modern Societies* (Stanford, CA, 1992), pp. 62–3, 94, 63, 137.
47 Jacqui Gabb and Janet Fink, *Couple Relationships in the 21st Century* (Basingstoke, 2015), esp. chap. 2.
48 Alain de Botton, "Why You Will Marry the Wrong Person," *New York Times* (May 28, 2016), at https://nyti.ms/2NopgCs. He elaborates on the point in bit.ly/3yGZbSv.
49 Allison Dunatchik, Kathleen Gerson, Jennifer Glass, Jerry A. Jacobs, and Haley Stritzel, "Gender, Parenting, and the Rise of Remote Work during the Pandemic: Implications for Domestic Inequality in the United States," *Gender and Society* 20/10 (2021): 1–12, at p. 4.

Chapter 4 Obsession

1 Vivian Gornick, *Fierce Attachments: A Memoir* (New York, 1987), pp. 76, 203.
2 Lyrics at bit.ly/3fdhl4u © Pronto Music, Mijac Music, Quinvy Music Publishing Co; live performance and comments at bit.ly/3d6AXGx. The song's popularity is discussed in the Wikipedia article at bit.ly/3cRLYgM.
3 Plato, *Symposium*, trans. Alexander Nehamas and Paul Woodruff (Indianapolis, 1989), cited by section number.
4 Aristotle [?], *Problems* 30.1 (954a 30), in *The Complete Works of Aristotle*, ed. Jonathan Barnes (Princeton, NJ, 2014).

5 Galen, *Commentary on Epidemics 6*, pt 8, lemma 62c, trans. from the Arabic (the original Greek has been lost) by Uwe Vagelpohl, in *Corpus Medicorum Graecorum, Supplementum Orientale*, vol. V 3: *Galeni in Hippocratis Epidemiarum librum VI commentariorum I–VIII versio Arabica* (Berlin, forthcoming).

6 Catullus, *The Complete Poetry of Catullus*, trans. David Mulroy (Madison, 2002), cited by poem number.

7 Lucretius, *On the Nature of Things*, trans. Martin Ferguson Smith (Indianapolis, 2001), 4.1060–68, p. 129.

8 Ovid, *Love Poems* in *Love Poems, Letters, and Remedies of Ovid*, trans. David R. Slavitt (Cambridge, 2011), cited by book, poem number and line.

9 Ovid, *The Art of Love*, trans. James Michie (New York, 2002), 3.97–8, p. 117.

10 Ovid, Letter 7, in *Love Poems, Letters, and Remedies of Ovid*, cited by line number.

11 Ovid, *Remedies*, ibid., lines 64–5.

12 Vergil, *The Aeneid*, trans. Shadi Bartsch (New York, 2021), cited by book and line number.

13 Bernart de Ventadorn, "It is no wonder if I sing" (Non es meravelha s'eu chan), in *Troubadour Poems from the South of France*, trans. William D. Paden and Frances Freeman Paden (Cambridge, 2007), pp. 80–1.

14 For example, as sung by the Folger Consort, at bit.ly/3oDssOp.

15 La Comtessa de Dia, "I'll sing of him since I am his love" (A chantar m'er de so qu'eu non volria), in *Troubadour Poems from the South of France*, pp. 107–8.

16 Performed by Evelyn Tubb, Michael Fields, and David Hatcher at bit.ly/3fDyLtr.

17 Irving Berlin for the 1946 Broadway musical; hear
the original cast at bit.ly/3nwgmk7.

18 Maria de Ventadorn and Gui d'Ussel, "Gui d'Ussel,
I am concerned" (Gui d'ussel, be.m pesa de vos),
in *Troubadour Poems from the South of France*,
pp. 129–30.

19 Hartmann von Aue, *The Complete Works of
Hartmann von Aue*, trans. Frank Tobin, Kim
Vivian, and Richard H. Lawson (University Park,
PA, 2001), pp. 46–7.

20 Walther von der Vogelweide, "Can anyone tell me
what love is?" (Saget mir ieman, waz ist minne?),
trans. Will Hasty, in Marion E. Gibbs and Sidney
M. Johnson, eds, *Medieval German Literature* (New
York, 1997), p. 271.

21 Giacomo da Lentini, "My lady, I wish to tell you"
(Madonna, dir vo voglio), in *The Poetry of the
Sicilian School*, ed. and trans. Frede Jensen (New
York, 1986), p. 3.

22 Giacomo, "Just like the butterfly, which has such
a nature" (Sì como 'l parpaglion ch'ha tal natura),
ibid., pp. 36–7.

23 Guido Guinizelli, "Love seeks its dwelling always
in the noble heart" (Al cor gentil rempaira sempre
amore), in Frederick Goldin, ed. and trans., *German
and Italian Lyrics of the Middle Ages: An Anthology
and a History* (Garden City, NY, 1973), pp. 287–
91.

24 Petrarch, "Aspro core et selvaggio et cruda voglia"
(A harsh heart and wild cruel desire), in *Petrarch's
Lyric Poems: The* Rime sparse *and Other Lyrics*, ed.
and trans. Robert M. Durling (Cambridge, 1976),
p. 434 (Poem 265); a Naxos recording of Willaert's
setting is available at bit.ly/3lkXpio.

25 La Comtessa de Dia, "I have been in heavy grief"
(Estat ai en greu cossirier), in *Troubadour Poems
from the South of France*, p. 110.

26 Chrétien de Troyes, *Erec and Enide*, trans. Dorothy Gilbert (Berkeley, CA, 1992), cited by line number.

27 Hartmann von Aue, *Iwein*, trans. Richard H. Lawson, in *The Complete Works of Hartmann von Aue*, cited by the first line number of the strophe.

28 Béroul, *The Romance of Tristran*, ed. and trans. Norris J. Lacy (New York, 1989), lines 2323–30.

29 Gottfried von Strassburg, *Tristan*, trans. A. T. Hatto (Harmondsworth, 2004), p. 44.

30 Chrétien de Troyes, *Lancelot or, The Knight of the Cart*, ed. and trans. William Kibler (New York, 1984), lines 4674–9.

31 Andreas Capellanus, *The Art of Courtly Love*, trans. John Jay Parry (New York, 1960), 168–70, 172, 184–6.

32 Geoffrey Chaucer, *The Parliament of Fowls*, in *The Riverside Chaucer*, ed. Larry D. Benson (3rd edn, Boston, 1987), lines 308–9.

33 Baldesar Castiglione, *The Book of the Courtier*, trans. Charles S. Singleton (Garden City, NY, 1959), pp. 15–16.

34 Quoted in Marianna D'Ezio, "Isabella Teotochi Albrizzi's Venetian Salon: A Transcultural and Transnational Example of Sociability and Cosmopolitanism in Late Eighteenth- and Early Nineteenth-Century Europe," in Ileana Baird, ed., *Social Networks in the Long Eighteenth Century: Clubs, Literary Salons, Textual Coteries* (Newcastle upon Tyne, 2014), p. 182.

35 Johann Wolfgang von Goethe, *The Sorrows of Young Werther*, ed. David Constantine (Oxford, 2012), 19, 12–14, 33, 46, 48, 68, 41, 73, 3, 93, 105.

36 Mary Wollstonecraft Shelley, *Frankenstein* (1831), p. 107; pdf at globalgreyebooks.com.

37 All the sources cited here in connection with this case are from Mark Seymour, *Emotional Arenas: Life, Love, and Death in 1870s Italy* (Oxford,

2020), pp. 21, 91–112. For all the correspondence, I have added punctuation for clarity.

38 Heather A. Love, David P. Nalbone, Lorna L. Hecker, Kathryn A. Sweeney, and Prerana Dharnidharka, "Suicidal Risk Following the Termination of Romantic Relationships," *Crisis* 39/3 (2018): 166–74.

39 Helen E. Fisher, Xiaomeng Xu, Arthur Aron, and Lucy L. Brown, "Intense, Passionate, Romantic Love: A Natural Addiction? How the Fields That Investigate Romance and Substance Abuse Can Inform Each Other," *Frontiers in Psychology* (May 10, 2016), doi: 10.3389/fpsyg.2016.00687.

40 Kate Folk, "Out There," *New Yorker* (March 23, 2020), at bit.ly/34L7VZF.

Chapter 5 Insatiability

1 Plato, *Symposium*, trans. Alexander Nehamas and Paul Woodruff (Indianapolis, 1989), cited by section number.

2 Gregory the Great, *Moralia in Job* 3.45.89, ed. Marcus Adriaen (*Corpus Christianorum Series Latina* 143B) (Turnhout, 1985), p. 1611.

3 Origen, *The Song of Songs: Commentary and Homilies*, trans. R. P. Lawson (Westminster, MD, 1957), pp. 22–3.

4 Tribolet (?), "Us fotaires qe no fo amoros" (A fucker who was not in love), in *Troubadour Poems from the South of France*, trans. William D. Paden and Frances Freeman Paden (Cambridge, 2007), p. 238.

5 See William D. Paden, *Love and Marriage in the Time of the Troubadours*, forthcoming.

6 John Donne, "To His Mistress Going to Bed" [1654], Poetry Foundation, bit.ly/3396BAm.

7 Walter Ralegh [Raleigh], *The Discovery of the*

Large, Rich and Beautiful Empire of Guiana [1596] (London, 1848), p. 115.

8 Pietro Aretino, "I modi," sonnet 11, quoted and trans. Paula Findlen, in "Humanism, Politics and Pornography in Renaissance Italy," in Lynn Hunt, ed., *The Invention of Pornography: Obscenity and the Origins of Modernity, 1500–1800* (New York, 1996), pp. 69–70.

9 Pietro Aretino, Lettera 1.315 [1537], in *Epistolario aretiniano*, bks 1–2, ed. F. Erspamer (Milan, 1995), at bit.ly/2GE8kVD; quoted and trans. in Raymond B. Waddington, *Aretino's Satyr: Sexuality, Satire, and Self-Projection in Sixteenth-Century Literature and Art* (Toronto, 2004), pp. 26, 115.

10 Pietro Aretino, *Dialogues*, trans. Raymond Rosenthal (Toronto, 2005), pp. 55, 64, 52, 27, 42, 107, 161.

11 Michel Millot (?), *The School of Venus: The Ladies Delight, Reduced into Rules of Practice*, trans. Anonymous (1680), pp. 55, 11, 17, 28.

12 Margaret C. Jacob, "The Materialist World of Pornography," in Lynn Hunt, ed., *The Invention of Pornography: Obscenity and the Origins of Modernity, 1500–1800* (New York, 1996), pp. 157–282.

13 Samuel Richardson, *Pamela, or Virtue Rewarded* (New York, 1958), pp. 91, 476.

14 Adrian Williamson, "The Law and Politics of Marital Rape in England, 1945–1994," *Women's History Review* 26 (2017): 382–413; Rebecca M. Ryan, "The Sex Right: A Legal History of the Marital Rape Exemption," *Law and Social Inquiry* 20 (1995): 941–1001.

15 John Locke, *An Essay Concerning Human Understanding* 2.20.4, in *The Clarendon Edition of the Works of John Locke*, ed. Peter H. Nidditch (Oxford, 1975), at www.oxfordscholarlyeditions.

com: "Anyone reflecting upon the thought he has of
the delight that any present or absent thing is apt to
produce in him has the idea we call love."

16 John Cleland, *Memoirs of a Woman of Pleasure*, ed.
Peter Sabor (Oxford, 1985), pp. 116, 11–12, 22, 25,
108, 80, 64.

17 Choderlos de Laclos, *Dangerous Liaisons*, trans.
Helen Constantine (London, 2007), pp. 201, 104,
148, 181, 180, 349, 352.

18 Sade, *Philosophy in the Bedroom* in *The Complete
Marquis de Sade*, trans. Paul J. Gillette, vol. 1 (Los
Angeles, 1966), pp. 208, 209.

19 Sade, *The Marquis de Sade: The Crimes of Love:
Heroic and Tragic Tales, Preceded by an Essay
on Novels*, trans. David Coward (Oxford, 2005),
pp. xl–xlv.

20 Sade, *Philosophy in the Bedroom*, p. 209.

21 Johann Wolfgang von Goethe, *Faust: A Tragedy
in Two Parts with the Walpurgis Night and the
Urfaust*, trans. John R. Williams (Ware, 2007), cited
by line number.

22 Tirso de Molina, "The Trickster of Seville and His
Guest of Stone," trans. Roy Campbell, in *Life is a
Dream and Other Spanish Classics*, ed. Eric Bentley
(New York, 1985), pp. 152, 163, 173.

23 Molière, *Don Juan*, trans. Brett B. Bodemer, 2010 at
digitalcommons.calpoly.edu/lib_fac/54/.

24 W. A. Mozart and Lorenzo Da Ponte, *Don Giovanni*,
trans. William Murray (1961), at bit.ly/3jBZe9X.

25 [George Gordon] Byron, *Don Juan*, in *Lord Byron:
The Major Works*, ed. Jerome J. McGann (Oxford,
1986), cited by canto and stanza number.

26 Quoted in Paul Douglass, "Byron's Life and
His Biographers," in Drummond Bone, ed., *The
Cambridge Companion to Byron* (Cambridge,
2004), pp. 7–26, at p. 11.

27 Giacomo Casanova, *History of my Life*, trans.

William R. Trask, abridged Peter Washington (New York, 2007), pp. 199, 192, 211, 16–17, 20, 22.

28 *Commonwealth* v. *Sharpless*, 2 Serg. & Rawle 91 (Sup. Pa. 1815), at https://cite.case.law/serg-rawle/2/91/.

29 *Roth v. U.S.*, 354 U.S. 476 (1957).

30 Stendhal, *The Red and the Black*, trans. Robert M. Adams, ed. Susanna Lee (New York, 2008), pp. 75, 250.

31 Stendhal, *Love*, trans Gilbert and Suzanne Sale (London, 2004).

32 Stendhal, *The Red and the Black*, p. 417.

33 Andrew J. Counter, *The Amorous Restoration: Love, Sex, and Politics in Early Nineteenth-Century France* (Oxford, 2016), p. 13.

34 Stendhal, *The Life of Henry Brulard* [i.e. Stendhal], trans. John Sturrock (New York, 1995), pp. 19–20.

35 Gustave Flaubert, *Sentimental Education*, trans. Robert Baldick, rev. Geoffrey Wall (London, 2004), p. 8.

36 Michel Winock, *Flaubert*, trans. Nicholas Elliott (Cambridge, 2016), pp. 32, 77, 425, 427–8.

37 Richard von Krafft-Ebing, *Psychopathia sexualis*, trans. Franklin S. Klaf (New York, 2011), pp. 42, 35.

38 See Patricia Cotti, "Freud and the Sexual Drive before 1905: From Hesitation to Adoption," *History of the Human Sciences* 21/3 (2008): 26–44, at p. 32.

39 Sigmund Freud, *"Wild" Psycho-Analysis* (1910), pp. 222, 226; at bit.ly/3iKCFyV.

40 Sigmund Freud, *Observations on Transference-Love (Further Recommendations on the Technique of Psycho-Analysis III)*, in Ethel Spector Person, Aiban Hagelin, and Peter Fonagy, eds, *On Freud's "Observations on Transference-Love"* (London, 2013), p. 24.

41 Sigmund Freud, *Totem and Taboo: Resemblances*

between the Psychic Lives of Savages and Neurotics,
trans. A. A. Brill (New York, 1918), p. 167.

42 Freud, *Observations on Transference-Love,* p. 19.

43 Laura Kipnis, *Against Love: A Polemic* (New York, 2003), p. 27.

44 Pascal Bruckner, *Has Marriage for Love Failed?,*
trans. Steven Rendall and Lisa Neal (Cambridge, 2013).

45 Grace Gelder, "Adventures in Self Marriage," TED
talk (2016), at bit.ly/3loO9d3.

46 Larry Kramer, *Faggots* (New York, 1978), pp. 16,
20, 316, 349–51, 335, 363, 362.

Conclusion

1 Stendhal, *The Red and the Black,* trans. Robert
M. Adams, ed. Susanna Lee (New York, 2008),
pp. 286–7.

2 L. E. Angus and L. S. Greenberg, *Working with
Narrative in Emotion-Focused Therapy: Changing
Stories, Healing Lives* (Washington, DC, 2011).

Further Reading

Chapter 1 Like-Mindedness

For the *Symposium*, see Martha C. Nussbaum, *The Fragility of Goodness: Luck and Ethics in Greek Tragedy and Philosophy* (rev. edn, Cambridge, 2001). For Cicero's jaundiced view of emotions in general, see Margaret R. Graver, *Cicero on the Emotions: Tusculan Disputations 3 and 4* (Chicago, 2002). M. T. Clanchy, *Abelard: A Medieval Life* (Oxford, 1997), offers insights into both Abelard and Heloise. Montaigne's friendships are interpreted as part of his ambitious and essentially political life in Philippe Desan, *Montaigne: A Life*, trans. Steven Rendall and Lisa Neal (Princeton, NJ, 2017). Susan Lanzoni, *Empathy: A History* (New Haven, CT, 2018), discusses the development of the term "empathy" and its many ramifications. For a critique of the science of mirror neurons, see Ruth Leys, "'Both of Us Disgusted in *My* Insula': Mirror-Neuron Theory and Emotional Empathy," in Frank Biess and Daniel M. Gross, eds, *Science and Emotions after 1945: A Transatlantic Perspective* (Chicago, 2014), pp. 67–95.

Chapter 2 Transcendence

For the Roman family in late antiquity across the pagan/ Christian divide, see Geoffrey Nathan, *The Family in Late Antiquity: The Rise of Christianity and the Endurance of Tradition* (London, 2000). On the medieval mystical tradition of which Origen, Saint Bernard, and Marguerite Porete were but a part, see Bernard McGinn, ed., *The Essential Writings of Christian Mysticism* (New York, 2006), and, for a more panoramic view, Harvey D. Egan, *Soundings in the Christian Mystical Tradition* (Collegeville, MN, 2010). Marco Santagata, *Dante: The Story of His Life*, trans. Richard Dixon (Cambridge, 2016), provides a sober and clear-sighted account of the poet. For eighteenth-century parents and children, see Joanne Bailey, *Parenting in England, 1760–1830: Emotion, Identity, and Generation* (Oxford, 2012).

Chapter 3 Obligation

Susan Treggiari, *Terentia, Tullia and Publilia: The Women of Cicero's Family* (London, 2007), discusses Roman marriages from a woman's points of view. On the Jewish background to Paul, see David Instone-Brewer, *Divorce and Remarriage in the Bible: The Social and Literary Context* (Grand Rapids, MI, 2002). On medieval marriage, James A. Brundage, *Law, Sex, and Christian Society in Medieval Europe* (Chicago, 1987), is essential. For changing theories of Christian marriage, see John Witte, Jr., *From Sacrament to Contract: Marriage, Religion, and Law in the Western Tradition* (2nd edn, Louisville, KY, 2012). Sally Holloway, *The Game of Love in Georgian England: Courtship, Emotions, and Material Culture* (Oxford, 2019), explores English eighteenth-century love letters and tokens, while Katharine Ann Jensen, *Writing Love:*

Letters, Women, and the Novel in France, 1605–1776
(Carbondale, IL, 1995), takes up the place of love letters
in French life and literature. On nineteenth-century obligations, see Michael Grossberg, *Governing the Hearth:
Law and the Family in Nineteenth-Century America*
(Chapel Hill, NC, 1985). Claire Langhamer, *The
English in Love: The Intimate Story of an Emotional
Revolution* (Oxford, 2013), takes up the demands of
love in twentieth-century England. On the uncertain-
ties of modern love and the illusion of finding the right
"contract" to deal with them, see Eva Illouz, *The End
of Love: A Sociology of Negative Relations* (Oxford,
2019).

Chapter 4 Obsession

On the society of Provence, see Fredric L. Cheyette,
*Ermengard of Narbonne and the World of the
Troubadours* (Ithaca, NY, 2001). William M. Reddy,
*The Making of Romantic Love: Longing and Sexuality
in Europe, South Asia, and Japan, 900–1200 CE*
(Chicago, 2012), offers a provocative look at love
and desire across three medieval cultures. C. Stephen
Jaeger, *Ennobling Love: In Search of a Lost Sensibility*
(Philadelphia, 1999), traces the idea of ennobling love
in Western culture. For a Darwinian approach to love's
obsession, see Helen Fisher, *Why We Love: The Nature
and Chemistry of Romantic Love* (New York, 2004).
Elena Ferrante, *The Days of Abandonment*, trans. Ann
Goldstein (New York, 2005), a novel, tracks a modern
love that is ripped apart, obsessively dwelled upon, and
eventually reordered.

Chapter 5 Insatiability

For insatiable love in the ancient world, see Thomas K. Hubbard, ed., *A Companion to Greek and Roman Sexualities* (Hoboken, NY, 2014). Aretino's Venetian world is well described in Guido Ruggiero, *Binding Passions: Tales of Magic, Marriage, and Power at the End of the Renaissance* (New York, 1993). On the importance of novels in the development of fantasies of love, see Ruth Perry, *Women, Letters and the Novel* (New York, 1980). Jad Smith, "How Fanny Comes to Know: Sensation, Sexuality, and the Epistemology of the Closet in Cleland's *Memoirs*," *The Eighteenth Century* 44/2–3 (2003): 183–202, discusses the influence of Locke on Cleland. Elizabeth M. Butler, *The Fortunes of Faust* (University Park, PA, 1998), traces the intertwined stories of Faust and Don Juan. The many early versions of Juan include the play by Molière (bit.ly/3b39EMm) and an opera by Giuseppe Gazzaniga with librettist Giovanni Bertati (bit.ly/3bc2q8X).

Bibliography

Abelard and Heloise, *The Letters and Other Writings*, trans. William Levitan. Indianapolis, 2007.

Aelred of Rievaulx, *A Rule of Life for a Recluse*, trans. Mary Paul Macpherson, in *Treatises* and *The Pastoral Prayer* trans. Mary Paul Macpherson. Spencer, MA, 1971.

_____, *Spiritual Friendship*, trans. Lawrence C. Braceland. Collegeville, MN, 2010.

Ambrose, Isaac, *The Well-Ordered Family*. Boston, 1762.

Andreas Capellanus, *The Art of Courtly Love*, trans. John Jay Parry. New York, 1960.

Angus, L. E., and L. S. Greenberg, *Working with Narrative in Emotion-Focused Therapy: Changing Stories, Healing Lives*. Washington, DC, 2011.

Anonymous, *The Art of Courtship; or The School of Love*. London, ?1750.

Aretino, Pietro, *Dialogues*, trans. Raymond Rosenthal. Toronto, 2005.

_____, *Epistolario aretiniano*, bks 1–2, ed. F. Erspamer. Milan, 1995.

_____, "I modi," trans. Paula Findlen, "Humanism, Politics and Pornography in Renaissance Italy," in *The Invention of Pornography: Obscenity and the*

Origins of Modernity, 1500–1800, ed. Lynn Hunt. New York, 1996.

Aristotle, *The Complete Works of Aristotle*, ed. Jonathan Barnes. Princeton, NJ, 2014.

_____, *Nicomachean Ethics*, trans. Terence Irwin. 2nd edn, Indianapolis, 1999.

Augustine, *The Confessions of St. Augustine*, trans. Rex Warner. New York, 1963.

_____, *Letters*, Vol. 2, trans. Wilfrid Parsons. Washington, DC, 1953.

_____, *On the Trinity, Books 8–15*, ed. Gareth B. Matthews, trans. Stephen McKenna. Cambridge, 2002.

Baird, Ileana, ed., *Social Networks in the Long Eighteenth Century: Clubs, Literary Salons, Textual Coteries*. Newcastle upon Tyne, 2014.

Bauman, Zygmunt, *Liquid Love: On the Frailty of Human Bonds*. Cambridge, 2003.

Baxter, Richard, *A Christian Directory*, vol. 3. London, 1825.

Bernard of Clairvaux, *On the Song of Songs*, trans. Kilian Walsh, vols. 1 and 2. Kalamazoo, MI, 1971, 1976.

Bernart de Ventadorn, "It is no wonder if I sing" (Non es meravelha s'eu chan), in *Troubadour Poems from the South of France*, trans. William D. Paden and Frances Freeman Paden. Cambridge, 2007.

Béroul, *The Romance of Tristran*, ed. and trans. Norris J. Lacy. New York, 1989.

Bone, Drummond, ed., *The Cambridge Companion to Byron*. Cambridge, 2004.

Botton, Alain de, "Why You Will Marry the Wrong Person," *New York Times*, May 28, 2016, https://nyti.ms/2NopgCs.

Bourke, Joanna, *Fear: A Cultural History*. Emeryville, CA, 2005.

Bray, Alan, *The Friend*. Chicago, 2003.

Bruckner, Pascal, *Has Marriage for Love Failed?* trans. Steven Rendall and Lisa Neal. Cambridge, 2013.

Byron, [George Gordon], *Don Juan*, in *Lord Byron: The Major Works*, ed. Jerome J. McGann. Oxford, 1986.

Casanova, Giacomo, *History of My Life*, trans. William R. Trask, abridged Peter Washington. New York, 2007.

Castiglione, Baldesar, *The Book of the Courtier*, trans. Charles S. Singleton. Garden City, NY, 1959.

Catullus, *The Complete Poetry of Catullus*, trans. David Mulroy. Madison, 2002.

Chagall, Bella, *First Encounter*, trans. Barbara Bray. New York, 1983.

Chaucer, Geoffrey, *The Parliament of Fowls*, in *The Riverside Chaucer*, ed. Larry D. Benson. 3rd edn, Boston, 1987.

Chrétien de Troyes, *Erec and Enide*, trans. Dorothy Gilbert. Berkeley, 1992.

_____, *Lancelot or, The Knight of the Cart*, ed. and trans. William Kibler. New York, 1984.

Christine de Pizan, *The Book of the City of Ladies*, trans. Earl Jeffrey Richards. Rev. edn, New York, 1998.

Cicero, *Laelius on Friendship*, in *De senectute, de amicitia, de divinatione*, trans. William Armistead Falconer. Cambridge, 1923.

_____, *Letters to Atticus*, ed. and trans. D. R. Shackleton Bailey, vol 1: *68–59 BC*. Cambridge, 1965.

_____, *Selected Letters*, trans. P. G. Walsh. Oxford, 2008.

Cleland, John, *Memoirs of a Woman of Pleasure*, ed. Peter Sabor. Oxford, 1985.

Comtessa de Dia, "I have been in heavy grief" (Estat ai en greu cossirier), in *Troubadour Poems from the South of France*, trans. William D. Paden and Frances Freeman Paden. Cambridge, 2007.

_____, "I'll sing of him since I am his love" (A

chantar m'er de so qu'eu non volria), in *Troubadour Poems from the South of France*, trans. William D. Paden and Frances Freeman Paden. Cambridge, 2007.

Coontz, Stephanie, *Marriage, a History: How Love Conquered Marriage*. New York, 2005.

Cotti, Patricia, "Freud and the Sexual Drive before 1905: From Hesitation to Adoption," *History of the Human Sciences* 21/3 (2008): 26–44.

Counter, Andrew J., *The Amorous Restoration: Love, Sex, and Politics in Early Nineteenth-Century France*. Oxford, 2016.

Dante Alighieri, *The Divine Comedy*, trans. Charles S. Singleton, 3 vols. Princeton, NJ, 1970–5.

_____, *Vita nuova*, trans. Dino S. Cervigni and Edward Vasta. Notre Dame, IN, 1995.

D'Ezio, Marianna, "Isabella Teotochi Albrizzi's Venetian Salon: A Transcultural and Transnational Example of Sociability and Cosmopolitanism in Late Eighteenth- and Early Nineteenth-Century Europe," in *Social Networks in the Long Eighteenth Century: Clubs, Literary Salons, Textual Coteries*, ed. Ileana Baird. Newcastle upon Tyne, 2014.

Dhuoda, *Handbook for William: A Carolingian Woman's Counsel for her Son*, trans. Carol Neel. Washington, DC, 1991.

Didion, Joan, "The White Album," in *We Tell Ourselves Stories in Order to Live: Collected Nonfiction*. New York, 2006.

Donne, John, "To His Mistress Going to Bed" [1654], Poetry Foundation, bit.ly/3396BAm.

Douglass, Paul, "Byron's Life and His Biographers," in Drummond Bone, ed., *The Cambridge Companion to Byron*. Cambridge, 2004.

Dunatchik, Allison, Kathleen Gerson, Jennifer Glass, Jerry A. Jacobs, and Haley Stritzel, "Gender, Parenting, and the Rise of Remote Work during the

Pandemic: Implications for Domestic Inequality in the United States," *Gender and Society* 20/10 (2021): 1–12

Duncan, Anne, "The Roman *Mimae*: Female Performers in Ancient Rome," in Jan Sewell and Clare Smout, eds, *The Palgrave Handbook of the History of Women on Stage*. Cham, 2020.

Elliott [Belson], Mary, *My Father: A Poem Illustrated with Engravings*. Philadelphia, 1817.

Eustace, Nicole, *Passion Is the Gale: Emotion, Power, and the Coming of the American Revolution*. Chapel Hill, NC, 2008.

Ferrante, Elena, *My Brilliant Friend*, trans. Ann Goldstein. New York, 2012.

Findlen, Paula, "Humanism, Politics and Pornography in Renaissance Italy," in *The Invention of Pornography: Obscenity and the Origins of Modernity, 1500–1800*, ed. Lynn Hunt. New York, 1996.

Fisher, Helen E., Xiaomeng Xu, Arthur Aron, and Lucy L. Brown, "Intense, Passionate, Romantic Love: A Natural Addiction? How the Fields That Investigate Romance and Substance Abuse Can Inform Each Other," *Frontiers in Psychology*, May 10, 2016, doi: 10.3389/fpsyg.2016.00687.

Flaubert, Gustave, *Madame Bovary*, trans. Lowell Bair. New York, 1972.

_____, *Sentimental Education*, trans. Robert Baldick, rev. Geoffrey Wall. London, 2004.

Folk, Kate, "Out There," *New Yorker*, March 23, 2020.

Frankfurt, Harry G., *The Reasons of Love*. Princeton, NJ, 2006.

Freeman, Kathleen, *The Murder of Herodes and Other Trials from the Athenian Law Courts*. Indianapolis, 1994.

Freud, Sigmund, *Observations on Transference-Love (Further Recommendations on the Technique of*

Psycho-analysis III), in *On Freud's "Observations on Transference-Love,"* ed. Ethel Spector Person, Aiban Hagelin, and Peter Fonagy. London, 2013.

_____, *Totem and Taboo: Resemblances between the Psychic Lives of Savages and Neurotics*, trans. A. A. Brill. New York, 1918.

_____, *"Wild" Psycho-Analysis*. 1910, bit.ly/3iKCFyV.

Gabb, Jacqui, and Janet Fink, *Couple Relationships in the 21st Century*. Basingstoke, 2015.

Galen, *Commentary on Epidemics 6*, trans. Uwe Vagelpohl in *Corpus Medicorum Graecorum, Supplementum Orientale*, vol. V 3: *Galeni in Hippocratis Epidemiarum librum VI commentariorum I-VIII versio Arabica*. Berlin, forthcoming.

Gálvez-Muñoz, Lina, Paula Rodríguez-Modroño, and Mónica Domínguez-Serrano, "Work and Time Use by Gender: A New Clustering of European Welfare Systems," *Feminist Economics* 17/4 (2011): 125–57.

Giacomo da Lentini, "Just like the butterfly, which has such a nature" (Sì como 'l parpaglion ch'ha tal natura), in *The Poetry of the Sicilian School*, ed. and trans. Frede Jensen. New York, 1986.

_____, "My lady, I wish to tell you" (Madonna, dir vo voglio), in *The Poetry of the Sicilian School*, ed. and trans. Frede Jensen. New York, 1986.

Gibbs, Marion E., and Sidney M. Johnson, eds, *Medieval German Literature*. New York, 1997.

Giddens, Anthony, *The Transformation of Intimacy: Sexuality, Love and Eroticism in Modern Societies*. Stanford, CA, 1992.

Glyn, Elinor, *The Philosophy of Love*. Auburn, NY, 1923.

Goethe, Johann Wolfgang von, *Faust: A Tragedy in Two parts with the Walpurgis Night and the Urfaust*, trans. John R. Williams. Ware, 2007.

_____, *The Sorrows of Young Werther*, ed. David Constantine. Oxford, 2012.

Goldin, Frederick, ed. and trans., *German and Italian Lyrics of the Middle Ages: An Anthology and a History*. Garden City, NY, 1973.

The Good Wife's Guide: Le Ménagier de Paris, A Medieval Household Book, trans. Gina L. Greco and Christine M. Rose. Ithaca, NY, 2009.

Gornick, Vivian, *Fierce Attachments: A Memoir*. New York, 1987.

Goscelin of St Bertin, *The Book of Encouragement and Consolation [Liber confortatorius]*, trans. Monika Otter. Cambridge, 2004.

Gottfried von Strassburg, *Tristan*, trans. A. T. Hatto. Harmondsworth, 2004.

Gowing, Laura, Michael Hunter, and Miri Rubin, eds, *Love, Friendship and Faith in Europe, 1300–1800*. Basingstoke, 2005.

Gregory the Great, *Moralia in Job*, ed. Marcus Adriaen, in *Corpus Christianorum. Series Latina*. Vol. 143B. Turnhout, 1985.

Guinizelli, Guido, "Love seeks its dwelling always in the noble heart" (Al cor gentil rempaira sempre amore), in Frederick Goldin, ed. and trans., *German and Italian Lyrics of the Middle Ages: An Anthology and a History*. Garden City, NY, 1973.

Hale, Rosemary Drage, "Joseph as Mother: Adaptation and Appropriation in the Construction of Male Virtue," in *Medieval Mothering*, ed. John Carmi Parsons and Bonnie Wheeler. New York, 1996.

Hartley, Gemma, *Fed Up: Emotional Labor, Women, and the Way Forward*. New York, 2018.

Hartmann von Aue, *The Complete Works of Hartmann von Aue*, trans. Frank Tobin, Kim Vivian, and Richard H. Lawson. University Park, PA, 2001.

Heffernan, Thomas J., ed. and trans., *The Passion of Perpetua and Felicity*. Oxford, 2012.

Hesiod, *Theogony* and *Works and Days*, trans.

Catherine M. Schlegel and Henry Weinfield. Ann Arbor, MI, 2006.

Hochschild, Arlie Russell, *The Managed Heart: Commercialization of Human Feeling*. Berkeley, CA, 1983.

_____, *Strangers in Their Own Land: Anger and Mourning on the American Right*. New York, 2016.

_____, with Anne Machung, *The Second Shift: Working Families and the Revolution at Home*. New edn, New York, 2012.

Homer, *The Odyssey*, trans. Peter Green. Oakland, CA, 2018.

Hugh of Saint Victor, *On the Sacraments of the Christian Faith (De sacramentis)*, trans. Roy J. Deferrari. Cambridge, 1951.

Hume, David, *A Treatise of Human Nature*, ed. David Fate Norton and Mary J. Norton. Oxford, 2001.

Hunt, Lynn, ed., *The Invention of Pornography: Obscenity and the Origins of Modernity, 1500–1800*. New York, 1996.

Iacoboni, Marco, "The Human Mirror System and its Role in Imitation and Empathy," in *The Primate Mind: Built to Connect with Other Minds*, ed. Pier Francesco Ferrari et al. Cambridge, 2012.

Jääskeläinen, Iiro P., Vasily Klucharev, Ksenia Panidi, and Anna N. Shestakova, "Neural Processing of Narratives: From Individual Processing to Viral Propagation," *Frontiers in Human Neuroscience* 14 (2020), doi: 10.3389/fnhum.2020.00253.

Jacob, Margaret C., "The Materialist World of Pornography," in Lynn Hunt, ed., *The Invention of Pornography: Obscenity and the Origins of Modernity, 1500–1800*. New York, 1996.

Jaeger, C. Stephen, *Ennobling Love: In Search of a Lost Sensibility*. Philadelphia, 1999.

Karant-Nunn, Susan, and Merry Wiesner-Hanks,

ed. and trans., *Luther on Women: A Sourcebook*. Cambridge, 2003.

Kaufmann, Jean-Claude, *The Curious History of Love*, trans. David Macey. Cambridge, 2011.

Kipnis, Laura, *Against Love: A Polemic*. New York, 2003.

Krafft-Ebing, Richard von, *Psychopathia sexualis*, trans. Franklin S. Klaf. New York, 2011.

Kramer, Larry, *Faggots*. New York, 1978.

Kurdek, Lawrence A., "The Allocation of Household Labor by Partners in Gay and Lesbian Couples," *Journal of Family Issues* 28 (2007): 132–48.

La Boétie, Étienne de, *Discourse on Voluntary Servitude*, in Montaigne, *Selected Essays*, trans. James B. Atkinson and David Sices. Indianapolis, 2012.

_____, *Poemata*, ed. James S. Hirstein, trans. Robert D. Cottrell, in *Montaigne Studies* no. 3 (1991): 15–47.

Laclos, Choderlos de, *Dangerous Liaisons*, trans. Helen Constantine. London, 2007.

Locke, John, *An Essay Concerning Human Understanding*, in *The Clarendon Edition of the Works of John Locke*, ed. Peter H. Nidditch. Oxford, 1975.

Love, Heather A., David P. Nalbone, Lorna L. Hecker, Kathryn A. Sweeney, and Prerana Dharnidharka, "Suicidal Risk Following the Termination of Romantic Relationships," *Crisis* 39/3 (2018): 166–74.

Lucretius, *On the Nature of Things*, trans. Martin Ferguson Smith. Indianapolis, 2001.

Lystra, Karen, *Searching the Heart: Women, Men, and Romantic Love in Nineteenth-Century America*. New York, 1989.

Maria de Ventadorn and Gui d'Ussel, "Gui d'Ussel, I am concerned" (Gui d'ussel, be.m pesa de vos), in *Troubadour Poems from the South of France*, trans. William D. Paden and Frances Freeman Paden. Cambridge, 2007.

May, Simon, *Love: A History*. New Haven, CT, 2011.

_____, *Love: A New Understanding of an Ancient Emotion*. Oxford, 2019.

McCallum, Jamie K., *Worked Over: How Round-the-Clock Work is Killing the American Dream*. New York, 2020.

McMahon, Darrin M., *Happiness: A History*. New York, 2006.

Millot, Michel (?), *The School of Venus: The Ladies Delight, Reduced into Rules of Practice*, trans. Anonymous, 1680.

Missale ad usum . . . Sarum, ed. Francis H. Dickinson. Burntisland, 1861–83.

Molière, *Don Juan*, trans. Brett B. Bodemer, 2010. digitalcommons.calpoly.edu/lib_fac/54/.

Montaigne, Michel de, *The Complete Works*, trans. Donald M. Frame. New York, 2003.

_____, *Les essais* [1595 edn], ed. Denis Bjaï, Bénédicte Boudou, Jean Céard, and Isabelle Pantin. Paris, 2001.

_____, *Selected Essays with La Boétie's Discourse on Voluntary Servitude*, trans. James B. Atkinson and David Sices. Indianapolis, 2012.

Mozart, Wolfgang Amadeus, and Lorenzo Da Ponte, *Don Giovanni*, trans. William Murray. 1961, bit.ly/3jBZe9X.

Newman, Barbara, ed. and trans., *Making Love in the Twelfth Century: "Letters of Two Lovers" in Context*. Philadelphia, 2016.

Origen, *The Song of Songs: Commentary and Homilies*, trans. R. P. Lawson. Westminster, MD, 1957.

Ovid, *The Art of Love*, trans. James Michie. New York, 2002.

_____, *Love Poems*, in *Love Poems, Letters, and Remedies of Ovid*, trans. David R. Slavitt. Cambridge, 2011.

Paden, William D., *Love and Marriage in the Time of the Troubadours*. forthcoming.

Paston Letters and Papers of the Fifteenth Century, Pt I, ed. Norman David. Oxford, 2004.

Person, Ethel Spector, Aiban Hagelin and Peter Fonagy, eds, *On Freud's "Observations on Transference-Love."* London, 2013.

Petrarch [Francesco Petrarca], *Petrarch's Lyric Poems: The* Rime sparse *and Other Lyrics*, ed. and trans. Robert M. Durling. Cambridge, 1976.

Plato, *Laws*, trans. Trevor J. Saunders, in *Plato: Complete Works*, ed. John M. Cooper. Indianapolis, 1997.

_____, *Symposium*, trans. Alexander Nehamas and Paul Woodruff. Indianapolis, 1989.

Plutarch, *Advice to the Bride and Groom* and *A Consolation to His Wife*, ed. and trans. Sarah B. Pomeroy. New York, 1999.

The Poetry of the Sicilian School, ed. and trans. Frede Jensen. New York, 1986.

Porete, Marguerite, *The Mirror of Simple Souls*, trans. Ellen L. Babinsky. New York, 1993.

Proulx, Annie, *Brokeback Mountain*. New York, 1997.

Ralegh [Raleigh], Walter, *The Discovery of the Large, Rich and Beautiful Empire of Guiana* [1596]. London, 1848.

Reeder, Ellen D., *Pandora: Women in Classical Greece*. Princeton, NJ, 1995.

Richardson, Samuel, *Pamela, or Virtue Rewarded*. New York, 1958.

Roberd of Brunnè [Robert Mannyng], *Handlyng Synne with the French Treatise on Which it is Founded, Le Manuel des Pechiez*, ed. Frederick J. Furnivall. London, 1862.

Robertson, [Hannah], *The Life of Mrs. Robertson ... A Tale of Truth as Well as of Sorrow*. Edinburgh, 1792.

Rose, Kate, *You Only Fall in Love Three Times:*

The Secret Search for Our Twin Flame. New York, 2020.

Rosenwein, Barbara H., *Anger: The Conflicted History of an Emotion.* London, 2020.

_____, ed., *Anger's Past: The Social Uses of an Emotion in the Middle Ages.* Ithaca, NY, 1998.

_____, *Emotional Communities in the Early Middle Ages.* Ithaca, NY, 2006.

_____, *Generations of Feeling: A History of Emotions, 600–1700.* Cambridge, 2016.

Rostowski, Jan, "Selected Aspects of the Neuropsychology of Love," *Acta Neuropsychologica* 7/4 (2009): 225–48.

Rotundo, E. Anthony, "Romantic Friendship: Male Intimacy and Middle-Class Youth in the Northern United States, 1800–1900," *Journal of Social History* 23 (1989): 1–25.

Rufus, Musonius, "What is the Chief End of Marriage?," in *Musonius Rufus: "The Roman Socrates,"* ed. and trans. Cora E. Lutz. New Haven, CT, 1947.

Ryan, Rebecca M., "The Sex Right: A Legal History of the Marital Rape Exemption," *Law and Social Inquiry* 20 (1995): 941–1001.

Sade, Marquis de, *Philosophy in the Bedroom,* in *The Complete Marquis de Sade,* trans. Paul J. Gillette, vol. 1. Los Angeles, 1966.

_____, *The Marquis de Sade: The Crimes of Love: Heroic and Tragic Tales, Preceded by an Essay on Novels,* trans. David Coward. Oxford, 2005.

Schaefer, David Lewis, ed., *Freedom over Servitude: Montaigne, La Boétie, and* On Voluntary Servitude. Westport, CT, 1998.

Segal, Erich, *Love Story.* New York, 1970.

Seymour, Mark, *Emotional Arenas: Life, Love, and Death in 1870s Italy.* Oxford, 2020.

Shelley, Mary Wollstonecraft, *Frankenstein.* 1831, globalgreyebooks.com.

Smith-Rosenberg, Carroll, "The Female World of Love and Ritual: Relations between Women in Nineteenth-Century America," *Signs* 1 (1975): 1–29.

Stehling, Thomas, *Medieval Latin Poems of Male Love and Friendship.* New York, 1984.

Stendhal, *The Life of Henry Brulard*, trans. John Sturrock. New York, 1995.

_____, *Love*, trans. Gilbert Sale and Suzanne Sale. London, 2004.

_____, *The Red and the Black*, ed. Susanna Lee, trans. Robert M. Adams. New York, 2008.

Stopes, Marie Carmichael, *Married Love: A New Contribution to the Solution of Sex Difficulties.* London, 1919.

Taylor, Ann, "My Mother," in Doris Mary Armitage, *The Taylors of Ongar.* Cambridge, 1939, bit.ly/36ySdTR.

Thucydides, *History of the Peloponnesian War*, trans. Rex Warner. London, 1972.

Tirso de Molina, "The Trickster of Seville and His Guest of Stone," trans. Roy Campbell, in *Life is a Dream and Other Spanish Classics*, ed. Eric Bentley. New York, 1985.

Titone, Fabrizio, ed., *Disciplined Dissent: Strategies of Non-Confrontational Protest in Europe from the Twelfth to the Early Sixteenth Century.* Rome, 2016.

Treggiari, Susan, *Roman Marriage:* Iusti Coniuges *from the Time of Cicero to the Time of Ulpian.* Oxford, 1991.

_____, "Women in Roman Society," in Diana E. E. Kleiner and Susan B. Matheson, eds, *I Claudia: Women in Ancient Rome.* New Haven, CT, 1996.

Tribolet (?), "Us fotaires qe no fo amoros" (A fucker who was not in love), in *Troubadour Poems from the South of France*, trans. William D. Paden and Frances Freeman Paden. Cambridge, 2007.

Troubadour Poems from the South of France, trans.

William D. Paden and Frances Freeman Paden. Cambridge, 2007.

Venarde, Bruce L., ed. and trans., *The Rule of Saint Benedict*. Cambridge, 2011.

Vergil, *The Aeneid*, trans. Shadi Bartsch. New York, 2021.

Waddington, Raymond B., *Aretino's Satyr: Sexuality, Satire, and Self-Projection in Sixteenth-Century Literature and Art*. Toronto, 2004.

Walther von der Vogelweide, "Can anyone tell me what love is?" (Saget mir ieman, waz ist minne?), in Marion E. Gibbs and Sidney M. Johnson, eds, *Medieval German Literature*. New York, 1997.

Williams, Craig A., *Roman Homosexuality*. 2nd edn, Oxford, 2010.

Williamson, Adrian, "The Law and Politics of Marital Rape in England, 1945–1994," *Women's History Review* 26 (2017): 382–413.

Winock, Michel, *Flaubert*, trans. Nicholas Elliott. Cambridge, 2016.

Wright, Thomas, ed., *Autobiography of Thomas Wright, of Birkenshaw, in the county of York, 1736–1797*. London, 1864.

Xenophon, *Oeconomicus: A Social and Historical Commentary*, trans. Sarah B. Pomeroy. Oxford, 1994.

Zucchino, David, and Fatima Faizi, "After Losing His Legs to a Bomb, Afghan Veteran Is on a New Journey," *New York Times*, January 26, 2020, nyti.ms/3okgbsv.

Figure Acknowledgments

The publishers would like to thank the following for permission to reproduce the following figures:

1. "Before I fight this dragon and rescue you, can I ask a few questions?" © Maddie Dai / The New Yorker Collection/ The Cartoon Bank, CondeNast; 2. 7th century Byzantium, Saints Sergius and Bacchus, icon, cold encaustic on pine, gold leaf, 28.5 × 42 cm, Inv. 111 >KK, The Bohdan and Varvara Khanenko Museum of Art, photo: Victor Andreyev. Reproduced with permission © The Bohdan and Varvara Khanenko National Museum of Arts (Kyiv, Ukraine); 3. © Chagall, Marc (1887–1985): Birthday, 1915. New York, Museum of Modern Art (MoMA). Oil on cardboard, 31¾ × 39¼" (80.6 × 99.7 cm). Acquired through the Lillie P. Bliss Bequest. Acc. no.: 275.1949, © 2021. Digital image, The Museum of Modern Art, New York/Scala, Florence. ADAGP, Paris and DACS, London 2021; 4. Genesis initial, from Biblia Veteris Testamenti, c. 1263, Bayerische Staatsbibliothek München, Clm. 28169, fol. 5r; 5. Coffret (Minnekästchen), c. 1325–50. © Rogers Fund and The Cloisters Collection, by exchange, 1950. The Metropolitan Museum of Art; 6. Inscribed funerary relief of Lucius Aurelius Hermia and his wife Aurelia Philematium, 80 BCE. From a tomb in the Via Nomentana, Rome. © Alamy, British Museum; 7. Relief of the Holy Family, c. 1160–80. © Dodge Fund, 1940. The

221

Metropolitan Museum of Art; 8. The Lover Heard, c. 1785, Louis Marin Bonnet. © Bequest of Ella Morris de Peyster, 1957. The Metropolitan Museum of Art; 9. Gold ring with intaglio of seated woman and flying Eros, 2nd half of the 5th century BCE © Purchase, The Bothmer Purchase Fund and Lila Acheson Wallace Gift, 1994. The Metropolitan Museum of Art; 10. Le Roman de la Rose, Guillaume de Lorris and Jean de Meun. © Paris Bibl. nat. ms fr. 25526, fol. 106v; 11. Roundel with Scenes of the Attack on the Castle of Love, c. 1320–40. © The Cloisters Collection, 2003. The Metropolitan Museum of Art; 12. Perfume bottle. © George Ortiz Collection; 13. Allegory of America, c. 1587–89, Jan van der Straet, called Stradanus. © Gift of Estate of James Hazen Hyde, 1959. The Metropolitan Museum of Art; 14. Medaglia di Pietro Aretino, verso con testa di falli. Sailko, Wikimedia Commons; 15. George Gordon, Lord Byron, c. 1820. © The Milton Weil Collection, 1940. The Metropolitan Museum of Art.

Index

Goscelin of Saint-Bertin;
Heloise and Abelard;
lust; marriage; Plato,
Symposium
*Love seeks its dwelling always
in the noble heart (Al
cor gentil rempaira
sempre amore)* (Guido
Guinizelli), 118–19
Love Story, see Jenny and
Oliver (*Love Story*)
lovesickness, *see* love, theories
of, medical; Galen
Lucretius, 45, 105–7
lust, 80–1, 107, 138, 148, 157,
165, 175
Luther, Martin, 56; *see also*
Protestant(s)

Malcolm & Marie (film), 98–9
Mannyng, Robert, *Handling
Sin*, 84
*Many a person hails me
(Maniger grüezet mich
alsô), see* Hartmann von
Aue
Map of Tenderness, *see*
Scudéry, Madeleine de
Maria de Ventadorn, 114–15
Marie de Champagne
(countess), 125–6
marriage, figure 8
ceremony,
medieval, 66
self-marriage, 173
vows of, 66–7, 78, 94,
99–100, 113, 120, 173,
178–81
conjugal debt in, 83, 93
in classical Greece and Rome,
45, 71–9
in Homer, 11–12, 68–70
medieval Church and, 25, 45,
66, 79–81
modern, 95–100
nineteenth century, 92–3,
165–9

self-marriage, 173
see also Heloise and Abelard;
Jenny and Oliver (*Love
Story*)
martyrdom, 45–7, 92; *see also*
Perpetua (Saint)
May, Simon, 7, 61, 182
McMahon, Darrin M., 3
*Memoirs of a Woman of
Pleasure, see Fanny Hill*
Merteuil (Marquise de), *see
Dangerous Liaisons*
Minnesänger, see Hartmann
von Aue; Walther von
der Vogelweide
mirror neurons, 35–40
Mirror of Simple Souls, see
Porete, Marguerite
monks, 1, 28, 48–51, 57–8, 64,
87, 112, 178, 181; *see
also* Aelred of Rievaulx;
Bernard (Saint);
Cistercians; Cluny; Rule
of Saint Benedict
Montaigne, Michel de, 29–33,
36, 39–40, 115, 178,
180
Moode, Eliza (18th-century
young woman), 88–9
Moreau, Frédéric, *see* Flaubert,
Sentimental Education
Mother's Magazine, 59
Musgrove, Jeannie Field,
37–8; *see also* love,
friendship(s), modern
female
Musonius Rufus, 75

Nanna, *see* Aretino
Nausicaa (*Odyssey*), 11–12, 28,
160
Need, 42, 137, 153, 158, 175;
see also daemon(s)
Neoplatonism, 52, 56, 62–3; *see
also* Plato, *Symposium*
Nestor (*Odyssey*), 10–11, 18,
35